CHARLES F. STANLEY BIBLE STUDY SERIES

BECOMING EMOTIONALLY WHOLE

CHANGE YOUR THOUGHTS TO BE HAPPIER AND HEALTHIER

CHARLES F. STANLEY

THOMAS NELSON
Since 1798

Becoming Emotionally Whole
Charles F. Stanley Bible Study Series

Original edition copyright 1996 and 2008 by Charles F. Stanley.
Revised and updated edition copyright 2020 by Charles F. Stanley.

Published in Nashville, Tennessee, by Thomas Nelson. Thomas Nelson is a registered trademark of HarperCollins Christian Publishing, Inc.

All Scripture quotations are taken from the New King James Version.® Copyright © 1982 by Thomas Nelson. Used by permission. All rights reserved worldwide.

Thomas Nelson titles may be purchased in bulk for educational, business, fundraising, or sales promotional use. For information, e-mail SpecialMarkets@ThomasNelson.com.

ISBN 978-0-310-10556-5 (softcover)
ISBN 978-0-310-10557-2 (ebook)

First Printing February 2020 / Printed in the United States of America

CONTENTS

Introduction: Preparing for a Journey into Emotions   5

LESSON 1   Understanding Your Emotions   7

LESSON 2   God Created Your Emotions   19

LESSON 3   A Healthy Emotional Response to Life   33

LESSON 4   The Foundation for Healthy Emotions   45

LESSON 5   Seven Keys to Emotional Wholeness   59

LESSON 6   The Ache of Anxiety   69

LESSON 7   The Grip of Fear   81

LESSON 8   The Grindstone of Guilt   93

LESSON 9   The Acid of Anger   107

LESSON 10 The Reproach of Rejection   117

LESSON 11 The Longing of Loneliness   129

LESSON 12 The Defeat of Discouragement   141

Leader's Guide   155

Preparing for a Journey into Emotions

This book is intended for Bible study. My hope as you engage in this study is that you will turn again and again to your favorite version of the Bible—to highlight specific words, underline phrases, write in the margins, or circle verses that speak to you in a special way. My Bible is well marked with such dates, notes, and insights.

Bookstores these days are filled with numerous self-help books—many of which deal with the topic of this study on emotional well-being—but the Bible is the ultimate "help" book. However, the advice it offers leads not to self-help but to God's help. The Bible holds God's eternal wisdom about emotions and how we are to express them. So make your Bible your ultimate authority on emotions and how to communicate them.

This book can be used by you alone or by several people in a small-group study. At various times, you will be asked to relate to the material in one of the following four ways.

First, what new insights have you gained? Make notes about the insights you have. You may want to record them in your Bible or in a separate journal. As you reflect on your new understanding, you are likely to see how God has moved in your life.

Second, have you ever had a similar experience? You approach the Bible from your own unique background . . . your own particular set of understandings about the world that you bring with you when you open God's Word. For this reason, it is important to consider how your experiences are shaping your understanding and allow yourself to be open to the truth that God reveals.

Third, how do you feel about the material? While you should not depend solely on your emotions as a gauge for your faith, it is important for you to be aware of them as you study a passage of Scripture and can freely express them to God. Sometimes, the Holy Spirit will use your emotions to compel you to look at your life in a different or challenging way.

Fourth, in what way do you feel challenged to respond or to act? God's Word may inspire you or challenge you to take a particular action. Take this challenge seriously and find ways to move into it. If God reveals a particular need that He wants you to address, take that as His "marching orders." God will empower you to do something with the challenge that He has just given you.

Start your Bible study sessions in prayer. Ask God to give you spiritual eyes to see and spiritual ears to hear. As you conclude your study, ask the Lord to seal what you have learned so you will not forget it. Ask Him to help you grow into the fullness of the nature and character of Christ Jesus.

I encourage you to keep the Bible at the center of your study. A genuine Bible study stays focused on God's Word and promotes a growing faith and a closer walk with the Holy Spirit in each person who participates.

UNDERSTANDING YOUR EMOTIONS

IN THIS LESSON

Learning: What should I do with my emotions?

Growing: What is the purpose of emotions?

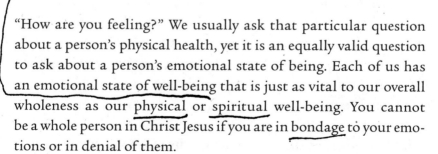

S P E F

"How are you feeling?" We usually ask that particular question about a person's physical health, yet it is an equally valid question to ask about a person's emotional state of being. Each of us has an emotional state of well-being that is just as vital to our overall wholeness as our physical or spiritual well-being. You cannot be a whole person in Christ Jesus if you are in bondage to your emotions or in denial of them.

I meet many people who try to deny they have an emotional response to the situations they encounter. They seem to believe that it is weak for a person to cry, a flaw for a person to feel anger to express disappointment, or a lack of self-control for a person to laugh aloud. Such people are missing out on the fullness of what it means to be alive.

An expression of emotion is part of what makes us human. Emotions are a gift of God, who created each of us with a capacity to feel and to express them. Furthermore, emotions are vital to our ability to communicate to others the uniqueness of our personalities. They are also a means of responding to God, to other people, and to life in general.

However, the problem is that many people don't know how to express their emotions in healthful ways that promote good relationships with friends and family members. Learning how to deal with one's emotions is a vital skill. We need to understand how to direct them toward good outcomes, express them without sinning, and give voice to our emotions in order to improve our communication with friends, family members, and others in our world.

Some people allow themselves to have a free-flowing emotional response to life and have learned to control their emotions, but they are uncomfortable talking about the way they feel. Learning how to tell others what you are feeling is a part of becoming a mature person. It is a skill that is critical to the development of adult-to-adult relationships.

Wherever you are on the spectrum of emotional growth—from denial to full expression—Jesus wants you to have emotional health. He wants you to express emotions in the way He created them to be expressed. He wants you to admit to emotions, to know how to control them and use them in right ways, and to discuss your emotional responses with others.

1. "To everything there is a season, a time for every purpose under heaven.... A time to weep, and a time to laugh; a time to mourn, and a time to dance" (Ecclesiastes 3:1, 4). What is a particular

S P E F

"season" of life that you are in right now? What type of emotions
is that bringing to the surface for you?

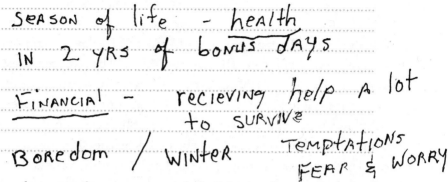

SeasoN of life - heAlth
IN 2 yRs of boNus dAys

FiNANCIAl - recieving help A lot
to SURviVe

BoReDom / WiNteR TempTATioNs
FEAR & WoRRy

2. In what areas have you struggled with certain emotions in the
past? How do you feel about expressing your emotions? About
discussing your emotions with others?

A pRiVAte peRsoN
do Not WANT To BuRDeN otheRs
HAVE opeNed uP too some
mAybe too muCH — to some
Feel hopeless At tiMEs
KNowiNg NothiNg is impossible
with God

EXPRESSING EMOTIONS

Are there good and bad emotions? Yes and no. Emotions in themselves are *neutral*. Their expression takes on the nature of good and
bad. All emotions are valid, and each has a place in God's design
of your human psyche and spirit. God created your emotions so you
might enjoy them and communicate to others by using them.

Each person is going to have a unique response to life's situations,
problems, and challenges. One person may weep at the beauty

9

of a moving piece of music, while another person may sit in silent awe, and yet still another person may stand to give thunderous applause. We must allow others the privilege of their expression.

We also must give one another the privilege of expressing emotions privately. I advocate the healthful and free expression of emotions, yet I do not believe that a person should be required to express emotions in the presence of others. Conversely, we must be careful not to assume we have the right to express our emotions freely and fully in the presence of others. Every public expression of emotion should take into consideration the people witnessing the emotional display. Courtesy and respect should govern our behavior. As we will discuss in this study, restraint is not denial of emotions. It is control of them in the presence of others.

The Bible is filled with stories of people who expressed their emotions in both good and bad ways. But perhaps no book in Scripture contains more heart-felt emotions than the Psalms. King David, in particular, wrote a number of these songs and poems that express a wide range of emotions. Consider the following sampling of just a few of these emotions from Psalms:

- Joy: "You have put gladness in my heart, more than in the season that their grain and wine increased" (Psalm 4:7).
- Peace: "I will both lie down in peace, and sleep; for You alone, O LORD, make me dwell in safety" (Psalm 4:8).
- Grief: "My eye wastes away because of grief; it grows old because of all my enemies" (Psalm 6:7).
- Anger: "How long, O LORD? Will You forget me forever? How long will You hide Your face from me?" (Psalm 13:1).
- Love: "I will love You, O LORD, my strength" (Psalm 18:1).
- Fear: "I sought the LORD, and He heard me, and delivered me from all my fears" (Psalm 34:4).
- Loneliness: "Turn Yourself to me, and have mercy on me, for I am desolate and afflicted" (Psalm 25:16).

- Hope: "Let Your mercy, O LORD, be upon us, just as we hope in You" (Psalm 33:22).
- Regret: "I am ready to fall, and my sorrow is continually before me. For I will declare my iniquity; I will be in anguish over my sin" (Psalm 38:17–18).
- Discouragement: "Why are you cast down, O my soul? And why are you disquieted within me?" (Psalm 42:5).
- Shame: "My dishonor is continually before me, and the shame of my face has covered me" (Psalm 44:15).

Sometimes we are overcome with emotion. We may lose control in a particular situation. At those times, we may feel that we should apologize for our lack of restraint, but we should never apologize for having feelings. After all, none of the psalmists held back in expressing their full range of human emotions to God. When we apologize for having emotions, we are in danger of stuffing them, with a possible eruption later. As we will discuss in future lessons in the study, stuffed emotions can only be damaging.

3. How do you respond to the idea that emotions are *neutral*—that they are neither inherently good nor bad? What makes it difficult to accept this truth?

11 TOP EMOTIONS

AGREE - they ARE NEUTRAL

NOT either good or bad

@ example (HOPE) your hope in what

OR IN whom — your desire - good or bad

4. As you look at the list of emotions expressed in the book of Psalms, which sentiment can you relate to the most right now? What are some emotions you need to express to God in prayer?

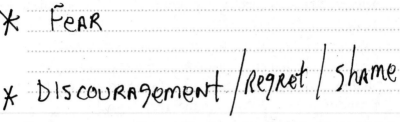

✗ Fear

✗ Discouragement / Regret / Shame

PURSUING EMOTIONAL WHOLENESS

From the outset, I want to establish that the goal of embarking on this journey is to lead you to a place where you can become emotionally whole. With this in mind, we will first explore how God created emotions, examine the foundation for building healthy emotions, and then look at how you can deal with specific emotions, including fear, guilt, anger, rejection, loneliness, and discouragement. In everything, the goal is to get you to a better place in your life—so you can be at peace with yourself, with others, and with God.

Let me ask you this question: *Is there something in your life that you prefer over contentment?* If so, you can stop reading this study at this point . . . and, while you are at it, stop asking God to make you content. If you are resolved to hold on to negative emotions like anger, fear, and discouragement—and refuse to forgive those who have wronged you—then you will not be able to get to this place of contentment and peace in your life.

However, if you are ready to move toward emotional wholeness—and engage with this study—then let me give you an overview of how we are going to proceed. *The first practical step begins with repenting of any sin that is keeping you from having a right standing with God and experiencing His joy and peace.* One of the roles of the Holy Spirit is to convict you of sin (see John 16:8), so you will be in a state of conflict until you yield to Him. Repent to God.

Second, rebuild your thought structures. What do I mean by this? You need to begin to think about your life with God at the center . . . and not yourself. There is no such thing as being contented and emotionally healthy when your entire life is revolving around you and the only thing that matters in your life is just you. There is no such thing as selfishness and contentment possessing the same heart. You have to rebuild your thought structure, get God into the center of your thinking, and interpret your life in the light of what He wants.

You say, "That will not be a quick or easy process." This is exactly right. I will not be providing any push-pull, click-click, turn-on-the-button, turn-it-off answers in this study, because no single emotion can be corrected overnight. So when I say rebuild your thought structures, I'm talking about you beginning to back off and look at the way you've been thinking about your life. God needs to be the *hub* of your life, because when this happens, you begin to relate Him to all aspects of your life. He is your Father. He is your provider. You can rely on Him. He is your loving heavenly Father who has already provided what you need. He is faithful.

Third, refocus your emotions. It is critical for you to refocus your emotions on God. "Lord, I want to love You. I want to honor You. I want to praise You. Lord, I want such a hunger in my heart for You that whatever else You send me, I'm going to leave that to You—but what I really want in my heart is You. I want You to saturate and permeate and color every single emotional desire of my life. I want it to be filtered through You."

Here is what we do all too often. We get up in the morning and say, "Lord, thank You for a good night's rest. Please bless my family today. Bless me on my job. I want to meet that financial need today." When we get through praying, we might as well have not even had time with God. What we really did was focus our emotions on the things God provides. As a result, we miss *Him.* That will never produce contentment and emotional wholeness in life. God isn't about to allow you to be content by ignoring Him.

Fourth, redirect your goals. You likely have many goals, and it is great to have them, because accomplishment is part of what God wants to do. But you need to redirect your goals so the primary one is to discover the will of God for you. Once that becomes the number one goal, it becomes easy to relate to Him and see Him as your provider. As we will discuss, many of our negative emotions come from a basic mistrust in God's faithfulness to provide for our needs. As we learn to trust God, we learn to surrender our lives and emotions to Him.

Finally, reproduce your life in someone else. It is interesting that in the Bible, God is always admonishing His followers to share their testimony. You can come to church, not miss a single service, give triple your tithe, read your Bible, pray, sing in the choir, and do anything else—but you will not find wholeness and contentment if you do not open yourself up to others. You will just be a locked-in lake that is quickly becoming a stagnant pool. Instead, your life needs to be a stream through with God is able to move and flow.

5. What are some negative emotions that you know you need to address in order to move into wholeness?

> FEAR

6. Are you willing to let those go? Why or why not?

> yes — but struggling
>
> Hope
> " He will do it again "

7. Which of the steps to contentment listed above especially stand out to you? What do you need to do to start moving toward putting that step into action?

Re focus your emotions

Love / Joy / Hope

UNCHARTED WATERS

For most of us, the realm of emotions has uncharted territories. We are unsure of the language of emotions. We have neglected or feared to explore areas of the inner life. Recognize at the outset of this study that if this is true for you, it is likely to be true for every other person that you know. Give family members, your circle of friends, other church members, your Bible study group, the freedom to err on their way toward emotional health.

God made you to have feelings. He wants you to experience His presence with your emotions, to express yourself emotionally, and to have an emotional relationship with other people. The Lord wants you to become emotionally whole!

8. What new insights about emotions do you think God may have for you personally?

Peace / Hope

9. In what areas do you feel challenged to grow emotionally as a means of becoming a more effective witness for Christ Jesus?

less WORRY

&

feAR

10. What are some specific things you hope to take from this study?

over come gRief

& dis couRAgemeNT

& feAR

TODAY AND TOMORROW

Today: God created all people with emotions, and they are a gift from Him to me.

Tomorrow: I will begin to recognize that there is nothing wrong with emotions—it is my response to them that matters.

CLOSING PRAYER

. . . .

Heavenly Father, thank You for creating our emotions. Today, we pray that we will not seek to hide or run from our feelings but start the process of embracing them and yielding them to Your control. Thank You for giving direction in our lives—for being our shield, our protection, and our provision. Help us to continually learn to trust in You in all things so that we know that we never have reason to fear, or be discouraged, or give in to anger . . . for You are always with us.

We never have reason to fear

Need not to fear discouragement

Ps 56

NOTES AND
PRAYER REQUESTS

Use this space to write any key points, questions, or prayer requests from this week's study.

ME — SPEF

DeBBie — depression
health /
feet

the lost

Temptations

GOD CREATED YOUR EMOTIONS

IN THIS LESSON

Learning: What difference does it make what I feel?

Growing: How can I learn to better control my emotions?

Where do our emotions come from? Are they a source of evil or good? People often ask me these questions. At times, they seem to imply that emotions are evil or that it is bad to exhibit certain emotions. But emotions are just part of our creation. God gave them to us.

The first few chapters of the Bible are filled with emotions. In Genesis 1, we see that creation arose from God's desire to have fellowship with humans—who were the culmination of His creation of the universe. Genesis 2 introduces the concept of loneliness. The Lord says about Adam, "It is not good that man should be alone; I will make him a helper comparable to him" (Genesis 2:18). In Genesis 3, we see Adam and Eve experiencing fear. When Adam hears God calling to him, he responds, "I heard Your voice in the garden, and I was afraid because I was naked; and I hid myself" (Genesis 3:10). *Desire, loneliness,* and *fear* are three of our most basic emotions . . . and they all appear in the opening verses of the Bible.

The fruit of the Holy Spirit—the character qualities the Holy Spirit manifests in our lives—are also emotion-laden: *love, joy, peace, longsuffering, kindness, goodness, faithfulness, gentleness,* and *self-control* (see Galatians 5:22–23). The Holy Spirit has chosen our emotions as His means of expressing Himself in our lives. Conversely, when Paul identifies the works of the flesh, he includes both emotions and behaviors (see Galatians 5:19–21).

Paul also writes, "Those who are Christ's have crucified the flesh with its passions and desires" (Galatians 5:24). Some people believe Paul is instructing us to crucify *all* our passions and desires, but this isn't what Paul is stating. Rather, he says those who are in Christ are to have crucified the *flesh*—the fleshly display of passions and desires that Paul terms "works of the flesh." We *are* to crucify hatred, jealousy, envy, and emotions related to selfish ambition and outbursts of anger. But we are *not* to crucify our emotions as a whole.

In a general sense, our emotions are neutral—they can be turned to good or evil. Our goal as Christians is to control our emotions so we manifest them in ways that build up others and ourselves. After all, God would not have given us something inherently bad. Yes, we can allow our emotions to run amok to the point they result in sinful behavior. We can allow our emotions to have free rein over our will. But the same emotions can also be turned toward Christ and be used to display godly behavior. God gave us emotions to *serve* us, not master us.

1. "But the fruit of the Spirit is love, joy, peace, longsuffering, kindness, goodness, faithfulness, gentleness, self-control. Against such there is no law" (Galatians 5:22–23). What emotions are involved in exhibiting love, joy, and peace?

....

....

....

....

....

....

....

....

2. What emotions are involved in exhibiting longsuffering, kindness, and goodness?

....

....

....

....

....

....

....

....

....

THE PURPOSE OF OUR EMOTIONS

Paul wrote these words of encouragement: "For God has not given us a spirit of fear, but of power and of love and of a sound mind" (2 Timothy 1:7). The Lord wants us to be filled with the power of the Holy Spirit and the emotion of love. He wants us to have the self-control (sound mind) to make wise choices about how we will display the power of the Holy Spirit with love.

God gave us emotions for positive reasons—the foremost being to prompt us to act. We may *think* a certain behavior is the right thing to do, but until we *feel* something in regard to that behavior, we may not act. For example, people know it is dangerous to drive when tired. They may think, "I shouldn't drive," yet continue driving. But if they doze for a second and awaken to find themselves inches from going into a ravine, they are likely to experience fear. That fear will be a literal wake-up call: "Pull off and get some rest, or you'll be in big trouble!"

Emotions mobilize us into action. *Fear* mobilizes us to protect ourselves. (This is not a spiritual fear, but the normal emotion of fear, such as fear of falling, fear of danger, and so forth.) *Anger* mobilizes us to correct wrongs—both those done against us and those done against loved ones. *Love* compels us to relate to one another and to God, to fulfill the needs of others, and to fulfill our need for satisfaction and meaning in life. *Desire* mobilizes us to get the things that we need for our psychological, emotional, and spiritual well-being.

When we manifest emotions in good behavior, the results include beauty, harmony, mutual benefit, and growth. When we manifest emotions in bad behavior, we encounter discord, estrangement, destruction, and sin. Furthermore, when we manifest emotions in right ways, we experience lasting enjoyment—the fun itself may be temporary, but it is a pleasure to recall. When we manifest emotions in wrong ways, we may experience temporary enjoyment, but the pleasure is fleeting and the memory of the occasion is painful.

The expression of emotion always has about it an element of pleasure or enjoyment. I have no doubt this is a second reason that God gave us emotions: so that we might experience pleasure, fun, good times, warm relationships, and satisfying feelings. God wants His people to enjoy life. The fruit of the Holy Spirit is expressed as *joy*! We are to delight in God's creation, in friendships, in marriage, and in all things. We are to enjoy the work and ministry opportunities that God puts before us. God has given us the emotional equipment necessary for experiencing pleasure, self-fulfillment, and self-satisfaction.

When we deny ourselves all opportunities to enjoy life, we miss out on the fullness of life that God desires. For too many people, pleasure has become equated with sin, but this isn't the way God designed life. He wants us to experience pleasure and to know how to have a good time *without* sinning. He wants us to be passionate people—especially in godly expressions of love and caring for others. He wants us to enjoy all that He gives us, does for us, and imparts to us and to respond with exuberant, energetic, joyful praise, thanksgiving, and acts of worship.

God never intended the Christian life to be stripped of emotions. Rather, we are to manifest a full, abundant, overflowing range of emotions in behavior that honors God and shows respect for others.

3. Consider the emotions *fear, anger, love,* and *desire*. Think about ways these emotions have compelled you to act in certain ways. Identify some of those behaviors—both the good and the bad.

Emotion	Good Behavior	Bad Behavior
Fear		
Anger		
Love		
Desire		

4. "So they went out quickly from the tomb with fear and great joy, and ran to bring His disciples word" (Matthew 28:8). This verse speaks of the disciples' reaction to Christ's resurrection. What did the disciples fear? What brought them joy? How did they express these emotions?

....

....

....

....

....

....

....

....

....

THE LINK BETWEEN EMOTIONS AND BEHAVIOR

Our emotions work in a basic way, common to both men and women. Emotions are attached to every thought. We have a way of "feeling" about every idea that we entertain. We allow a thought or idea to take root in our minds, we visualize that thought taking place in reality, and then we make a decision in the will about how to respond. The degree to which our emotions are a part of this process determines how quickly and how intensely we will act on the idea.

The Bible tells us the following about humankind: "As [a man] thinks in his heart, so is he" (Proverbs 23:7). What you allow yourself to think about gets you into trouble far more than your emotions do. It is your thought life that you are to govern with diligence. For this reason, avoid activities that you know are going to feed negative or sinful thoughts and images. Go out of your way to halt the flood of violent, seductive, and tempting messages that come to you.

Turn off the dial, turn away your eyes, turn down certain invitations, and you will be sparing yourself the agony of dealing with an overwhelming number of ungodly ideas. After all, once sinful images and ideas have entered into your mind, your emotions will be engaged regarding them. Your willpower will be required to make a decision about how to respond. It is much easier to avert or deny the input of negative and potentially harmful ideas than to exert willpower to keep from responding to them.

5. When have you found it difficult not to act on an idea that had rooted itself in your mind and engaged your emotions? From where did this idea originate?

....
....
....
....
....
....
....
....
....
....

6. When has a good idea taken root in your mind and emotions, leading to good actions? From where did that idea originate?

....
....
....
....
....
....
....
....
....

THE FOUNDATION FOR CONTROLLING EMOTIONS

As you read this Bible study, you will frequently find the word *control* linked to emotions. We will consider what *control* means, but first we need to examine four alternatives that people often take in responding to their emotions.

The first is to repress them. When people repress their emotions, they refuse to admit they have feelings. They may even deny the existence of one or more specific emotions—such as the fact they feel angry or discouraged or depressed. Repression is unhealthy, and it can lead to behaviors that cause harm to others.

A second response is to stifle emotions. When people have emotional responses but refuse to give them expression, they are stifling their emotions. They may have an "I can't" or an "I won't" orientation. They feel a deep agitation inside, but for either "can't" or "won't" reasons, they refuse to give expression to what they feel. The result is immense frustration. Some people refer to this as stuffing emotions inside. If people continue to stifle what they feel, they may find the emotions building to an eruption later in life, or they may find their pent-up emotions eating away at them, resulting in physical or psychological illness.

A third response is to drift away from emotions. Some people never pay attention to their emotions. They simply drift along, figuring they will come and go. If we experience emotions but don't deal with them, they can become entrenched in us and more firmly rooted in us. For example, if we are angry in one situation, but we never allow that anger to run its course, it can become the foundation for a pattern in our lives. The next time we are angry, the new anger builds on the previous anger, and resulting behavior may be more volatile or violent. Over time, we may become an angry person—ready to be ignited at any time. When emotions drift without control, they become deeply ingrained in the personality.

A fourth response is to pray for deliverance. I have met a number of people who choose to pray for deliverance from certain emotions rather than to face the fact they need to control their emotions. They want God to take away their capacity for anger, loneliness, fear, discouragement, and so forth rather than learn to deal with these emotions and grow in an ability to use them constructively in their lives.

Some people pray, "Lord, deliver me from impatience." That sounds like a good prayer, but consider what would happen if the Lord really did deliver you from impatience. You would lose your frustration at not having things done on your timetable and in your way, and you would probably lose any desire to pursue good goals. Your ambition would be squelched. You would allow many things to slide by unchallenged and uncorrected. You may easily become nonchalant in your attitude and lackadaisical toward sin. Rather than pray for deliverance from emotions, you need to pray for God to give you wisdom in how to deal with your emotions and how to control them in ways that are in keeping with His Word and His plan for your life.

7. How do you tend to respond to your emotions? If you have found yourself responding in any of the ways listed above, what negative effects have you seen in your life?

8. "'Be angry, and do not sin': do not let the sun go down on your wrath, nor give place to the devil" (Ephesians 4:26–27). Why does Paul say that anger is not sin? How can a person "be angry" without committing sin?

....

....

....

....

....

....

....

....

THE PROCESS OF CONTROLLING EMOTIONS

How, then, can you truly control your emotions? *First, experience the new birth in Christ Jesus.* You can't control your emotions by yourself. You need the help of the Holy Spirit—and His help is made available only to those who accept the sacrifice that Jesus Christ made on the cross. If you want to control your emotions today, ask Jesus to become the Lord of your life and fill you with His Holy Spirit. If you are already a Christian, ask the Holy Spirit to help you to control your emotions and change your emotional responses that may be damaging or in error.

Second, examine your dominant thoughts. What do you think about most often? What you think about today is what you become tomorrow. As you examine your thoughts, be aware of the feelings associated with them. If your dominant thought is about how a person has wronged you and what you might do in response, consider your feelings. Are you angry, disappointed, frustrated, or perplexed?

Your feelings are going to have a great impact on the course of action that you take.

Third, exchange thoughts and feelings that are contrary to God's Word. When you take inventory of your thoughts and the feelings associated with them, you may find that what you are thinking and feeling is *not* what would be pleasing to God. To know what is pleasing to God, of course, you need to have an understanding of what the Bible says. Once you have identified a thought pattern that is not in line with God's Word, ask the Lord to help you change the way you are thinking and feeling. Choose to make a different set of responses.

Of course, a change of this type takes patience, love, and a genuine desire to pursue a godly life. Identify what you would rather be thinking about. Identify the way you would like to feel. Be aware that, in deciding to think about something other than what has occupied your mind, you must select something that is pleasing to God. In identifying a new emotional response, you must choose something that is in keeping with God's plan and desire for you. Exchanging harmful thoughts and emotions for other equally harmful ones is certainly not what the Lords wants.

Fourth, exercise your privilege of prayer. Thank the Lord in prayer for changing your thoughts and feelings to conform with His Word and the life manifested by Jesus Christ. State your prayer in positive terms: "Thank You, Lord, for teaching me to trust, helping me to overcome, and giving me a new feeling as my automatic response toward this situation or person." Such a prayer can result in strengthening your faith and renewing your mind.

Finally, expect God's healing to begin immediately. You may not feel the Lord healing you of harmful thoughts and emotions immediately, but you can start *believing* in God's healing immediately. Believing is the forerunner of all spiritual realities. In turn, spiritual realities are the forerunner of all physical and material realities. You may not see the fullness of God's healing for some time, but you can expect and believe that God's healing has begun in you.

Why pray for healing of your thought patterns and your emotional responses? The reason is simply because emotional responses that are not controlled can bring about great harm in your life. They can result in physical ailments too numerous to recount, as well as psychological or mental illness. They can result in flawed, unhealthy, or shattered relationships. A failure to control your emotions can be devastating, especially if your errant emotions lead you to sin or cause others to sin. The end result of sin is death, both literally and figuratively.

The Lord instead desires for you to have strong, healthy emotions subjected to the control of the Holy Spirit at work in your life. The Lord created emotions for your good, and He desires that you draw benefit and pleasure from being a person who can have a "feeling" response to Him and to others. So make it your prayer today that you will ask the Lord to help you develop healthy emotions. Ask Him to give you the courage to exhibit your emotions in appropriate and healthy ways to the benefit of yourself and others.

9. "Everywhere and in all things I have learned both to be full and to be hungry, both to abound and to suffer need. I can do all things through Christ who strengthens me" (Philippians 4:12–13). What does Paul say is the secret to controlling emotions in all situations? How is this accomplished?

10. "Those who are Christ's have crucified the flesh with its passions and desires" (Galatians 5:24). What does it mean to "crucify the flesh"? How does a person crucify the flesh while still expressing emotions?

....

....

....

....

....

....

TODAY AND TOMORROW

Today: My emotions influence my behavior, and the Holy Spirit holds the key to controlling them.

Tomorrow: I will spend time each day asking the Lord to bring healing in my emotional life.

CLOSING PRAYER

Father, how grateful we are that You don't want us wasting away our life, sulking in our negative emotions and what we consider our failures in life. You want the best for us—and the decision is ours to take the first step that leads to a better life. We know that You encourage us to make the right choice . . . but ultimately it is our decision to make. Help us to actively embrace this process of seeking healing in our emotions. We open up our lives today to allow the work of the Holy Spirit to transform us into the people You want us to be.

NOTES AND
PRAYER REQUESTS

Use this space to write any key points, questions, or prayer requests from this week's study.

A Healthy Emotional Response to Life

Learning: When is it not appropriate for me to express my emotions?

Growing: How can I gain control over these feelings that I have?

"Emotions are good. Emotions are our friends. Emotions are a sign of strength. Emotions are to be encouraged." How often do you hear statements such as these? Probably not often. In most cases when emotions are discussed, they are couched in disparaging terms. They are regarded as something to be avoided or squelched. In this lesson, we're going to look at some of the false notions about emotions and what God's Word says about emotional health.

FALSE IDEAS ABOUT POSSESSING EMOTIONS

People have many erroneous ideas about emotions, which we will discuss in this section. One of the most basic errors is expressed in the statement, *"I'm just not an emotional person."* (Men often make this statement.) What the person really means is that he or she doesn't express emotions freely, properly, or in a healthy way. This person is missing out on a great deal of enjoyment in life. The fact is, *every* person is an emotional person. Each person is born with a capacity for having emotions and expressing them. Babies cry, smile, and respond to pleasure and pain. They become angry, show fear, or cuddle in response to love.

Proper expression of emotions refers to the match between an emotion and a behavior. It is proper to show grief by crying. It may also be proper to show anger or happiness by crying. Conversely, it is not proper to show grief by laughing. Some people have never learned the proper way to express their emotional response to the events they face in life, and because they are unsure of themselves, they deny themselves any expression of emotions.

Appropriate expression of emotions refers to the context in which an emotion is expressed. At some times and places, it may be inappropriate to express certain emotions. For example, dissolving into a puddle of tears before your boss or your employees may be inappropriate. Your decision not to express emotion at certain times or places, or in the presence of certain people, is not a denial of emotions but an example of controlling your emotions until you can express them fully in an appropriate setting or in the presence of people with whom you feel comfortable.

In the Gospels, we read that Jesus was an emotional person. The Bible offers numerous examples of His expressing different kinds of emotions. The actions of Jesus in the Gospel accounts show that He felt sorrow and grief, loneliness (or aloneness), frustration and anger, love and concern (compassion), and many more feelings along the full spectrum of emotions. Jesus knows what we feel because He has felt what we feel.

1. "Therefore, when Jesus saw her weeping, and the Jews who came with her weeping, He groaned in the spirit and was troubled. And He said, 'Where have you laid him?' They said to Him, 'Lord, come and see.' Jesus wept" (John 11:33–35). Why did Jesus weep in this instance? Do you think this was this an appropriate or inappropriate response?

2. How have you responded when confronted with another person's grief? How have you responded during your own times of grief?

OTHER COMMON ERRORS
ABOUT EMOTIONS

We will now look at some other common errors about emotions. *The first false idea is that expressing emotions is a sign of weakness.* The person who says this is usually uncomfortable with weakness. We are all weak at times. In my opinion, it is a strong and healthy person who expresses emotions, but it is a weak person who represses them. A person with extremely low self-esteem often has difficulty expressing emotions. It is not weak to cry in the privacy of your own room after a loved one has died, betrayed you, or abandoned you. It is not weak to admit that you have been angry, disappointed, frustrated, or lonely on occasion. It is not weak to tell your child that you love her and to do so with a hug.

In the Gospel of Luke, we read how Jesus sent seventy disciples out into the villages and cities to preach the gospel. When they returned, they said to Jesus, "Lord, even the demons are subject to us in Your name" (Luke 10:17). Luke writes that Jesus "rejoiced in the Spirit" (verse 21) when He heard the good report. He was willing to show others He was happy! I know people who don't show others that they are pleased or happy about something out of fear that someone may take advantage of them. Jesus never had that attitude. His rejoicing was not weakness. It was a spontaneous emotional response to good news.

A second false idea about emotions is that they are our enemies. People who say this may have been betrayed by their emotions when they failed to control them or when they expressed their emotions inappropriately. Our emotions are assets when they are controlled.

A third false idea about emotions is that they are unrelated to the human spirit. Nothing could be farther from the truth. Our emotions are closely linked with our spiritual development. We have opinions about God as well as feelings toward God—and the feelings that we have toward God are often much more basic and long-standing in our lives than our opinions. In fact, our opinions about God are often based on our feelings!

I tend to hear this statement from people who have sought out help from a professional counselor who did not have faith in Christ or desire to help others from a Christian perspective. If you are seeking counseling for any problem in your life, I would strongly advise you to find a Christian counselor. Every area of your life is linked to your spirit and to your faith—especially the areas with a strong emotional component. The more feelings associated with a problem, the greater your need for a *Christian* counselor.

A fourth false idea about emotions is that the best way to handle them is to let them all out. This approach may make the person feel better, but it is not the wisdom of God. We do not live unto ourselves. We are responsible for the way we behave in the presence of others. Again, we come back to *appropriateness.* Sometimes, certain emotions should not be expressed in the presence of certain people or under certain conditions. Learning when to let your emotions out and when to hold them in is a vital part of learning how to control your emotions. The person who continually inists on letting them all out is typically egocentric and uncaring.

3. Which of these false ideas have you held? Why is it important to not see emotions as a sign of weakness, view them as enemies, or seem them as unrelated to your spiritual development?

4. When have you indulged your emotions freely and "let them all out" in an inappropriate manner? What would have been appropriate in those circumstances?

....

....

....

....

....

....

....

....

....

....

....

GOD'S PICTURE OF EMOTIONAL HEALTH

Jesus is our role model for expressing emotions appropriately. He had perfect emotional health. In the Gospels, we see that He clearly displayed four basic tenets of emotional health. *First, He relied on God.* Jesus placed His trust squarely in the Father. He didn't rely on the religious structure of the day, the world's systems, or anything else to help Him accomplish His purposes. He relied on His heavenly Father for everything He needed.

To feel emotionally secure and healthy, you must place your total trust in God and believe that He will take care of you, protect you, and love you regardless of what anyone else says or does to you. You must rely on Him for your health, daily provision, strength, courage, and wisdom. You may be alone and experience temporary loneliness, but you can always know that God is present and that there is no greater friend than Jesus.

Second, Jesus gave generously to others. Jesus never withheld a miracle from anyone who asked Him for one. He freely preached the good news to all who were willing to hear. He was willing to risk pain and harm, even rejection and death, to make Himself available to all. The person with healthy emotions is willing to risk love. When you are emotionally healthy, you openly express care, concern, and compassion. The emotion of love is always manifested in some form of giving. The emotionally healthy person loves generously and gives generously in as many ways as possible, to as many people as possible, as often as possible.

Third, Jesus continually asked for the Holy Spirit's guidance. Everything that Jesus did was revealed to Him by the Father. You must likewise ask the Holy Spirit to reveal the Father's will to you. You may feel anger, for example, but by asking the Holy Spirit for guidance in how to channel that anger into positive behavior, you will find an outlet for anger that results in blessing instead of harm. Continual reliance on the Holy Spirit takes the form of continual prayer. To pray is to talk to God . . . and you are wise to talk to God around the clock, every day of the week (see 1 Thessalonians 5:17).

Fourth, Jesus recognized the true spiritual enemy. Jesus had numerous confrontations with people who denied His divinity, questioned His authority, and attempted to undermine His teachings and miracles. But Jesus always recognized that His true enemy was Satan. You will likewise have countless experiences in which you will feel negative emotions— hurt, anger, frustration, disappointment, worry, discouragement. Your first response may be to even the score with the person who has hurt you, but it is important to remember that ultimately the battle is not with the person but with the true enemy of your soul: the devil. So do not take revenge against others, but instead resort to prayer, to giving, and to blessing.

5. "A man who has friends must himself be friendly, but there is a friend who sticks closer than a brother" (Proverbs 18:24). What emotions are required if a person is to have friends? What should you do if you find yourself *without* friends?

....
....
....
....
....

6. "Give, and it will be given to you: good measure, pressed down, shaken together, and running over will be put into your bosom. For with the same measure that you use, it will be measured back to you" (Luke 6:38). What "measure" do you use when giving to others? What will result if you give more generously?

....
....
....
....
....

7. "Trust in the LORD with all your heart, and lean not on your own understanding; in all your ways acknowledge Him, and He shall direct your paths" (Proverbs 3:5–6). What does it mean to "lean on your own understanding"? What does it mean to acknowledge the Lord in all your ways? What effect will each of these have on your emotions?

....
....
....
....
....
....

8. "Put on the whole armor of God, that you may be able to stand against the wiles of the devil" (Ephesians 6:11). How does the devil use our emotions to harm us? How can we fight against this by putting on the "armor of God" (see Ephesians 6:14–18)?

....

....

....

....

....

....

....

A DESIRE FOR WHOLENESS

Are you willing to turn away from repressing your emotions and seek instead to control them? Do you desire to base your emotional health on the same principles reflected in the life of Jesus Christ? The first step toward emotional wholeness is to make a decision to pursue emotional health and strength, bringing your emotional life into harmony with your spiritual life—a whole life founded on Christ Jesus.

9. "I am the vine, you are the branches. He who abides in Me, and I in him, bears much fruit; for without Me you can do nothing" (John 15:5). What does it mean to abide in Christ? How does the analogy of the vine and branches illustrate the concept?

....

....

....

....

....

....

....

10. How does abiding in Christ influence your emotions? What practical steps are involved in this process?

....

....

....

....

....

....

....

....

....

....

....

....

....

....

....

....

....

....

TODAY AND TOMORROW

Today: Proper expression of emotions requires my deliberate decisions—and the Holy Spirit's help.

Tomorrow: I will pray that the Holy Spirit will make me more like Christ.

CLOSING PRAYER

Heavenly Father, we want to have a healthy emotional response to life. Please begin the healing process within us as we commit to yield those emotions that are out of control in our lives to Your control. We submit these emotions to Your will so they can enable us, as Your servants, to do the work of Your kingdom. We ask that the Holy Spirit will liberate us to express our God-given emotions in ways that bring joy, happiness, peace, contentment, and fulfillment. Let the people around us see the change in our emotions that only You can bring.

NOTES AND
PRAYER REQUESTS

Use this space to write any key points, questions, or prayer requests from this week's study.

THE FOUNDATION FOR HEALTHY EMOTIONS

IN THIS LESSON

Learning: How can I learn to love myself?

Growing: What is the difference between loving myself and being self-centered?

Do you like the person you see in the mirror? Liking yourself relates to self-image, which is not limited to your physical appearance. Self-image includes the total you—personality, talents, accomplishments, and relationship with the Lord. Your emotional health is rooted strongly in your self-image, as are your relationships with family members and friends. Nearly all of your behavior is based on who you think you are and how you feel about yourself.

THE BASIS FOR A HEALTHY SELF-IMAGE

Paul wrote an interesting statement to the believers in Corinth: "For I am the least of the apostles, who am not worthy to be called an apostle, because I persecuted the church of God. But by the grace of God I am what I am, and His grace toward me was not in vain; but I labored more abundantly than they all, yet not I, but the grace of God which was with me" (1 Corinthians 15:9–10). On the surface, Paul appears to be putting himself down. However, a closer reading reveals the exact opposite. Paul had a very healthy self-image!

This passage was part of Paul's response to the Corinthians, who were arguing about whether they should heed his words or listen to other teachers. At the beginning of 1 Corinthians 15, Paul reminded them that the gospel he had preached had resulted in their salvation: Jesus Christ died for their sins, was buried, and rose the third day—as witnessed by Peter, the apostles, five hundred followers of Jesus, and Paul himself.

Paul, in saying that he was "least" of all the apostles, was stating that he was the last among those who witnessed the resurrected Christ, and that of all those named, he spent the least amount of time with Jesus. But, Paul said, "by the grace of God I am what I am"—which was an apostle and an ardent follower of Jesus. Paul had spent a limited time with the Corinthians, but that wasn't what counted. What he *did* with the time mattered in God's eyes.

Paul also said that God's grace toward him was not in vain—that he had received Christ, that he had labored to witness to others, and that God's grace has continued to work through his life. This powerful statement from Paul reveals his strength of character and his strong self-image. Paul was not putting himself down. He was simply stating facts about his life—the foremost one of which was that everything he did was in keeping with God's saving grace.

Ultimately, your self-image is linked to who you are in Christ Jesus. If you have no relationship with Christ, it will be difficult for you to have a strong and healthy self-image. However, if you have a relationship with Christ, you have accepted the fact that God so loved you that He sent Jesus to die for your sins so that you could have eternal life (see John 3:16).

Do you know with certainty today that God loves you infinitely, unconditionally, and eternally? That He stands ready to forgive you of all your sins? That Jesus valued you so much that He gave His life so that you might live forever with Him in heaven? That you are being transformed more and more into the likeness of Jesus Christ as the Holy Spirit works in your life? If you can say yes to these questions, you have a firm basis for a healthy self-image.

Unfortunately, even those who believe that Jesus died for their sins sometimes have difficulty loving themselves. If God loves you and has forgiven you, you should love yourself. If God says that you are that valuable, you are! If the Holy Spirit of God is refining and perfecting you, surely you are a cherished child of God! Nobody can force you to see the truth of God's love in your life or make you accept the fact you are valuable to Him. You must paint on your mental canvas the image that reflects what you believe to be true about yourself. Your worth and self-image must flow from Christ Jesus. You are worthy because He declares you worthy.

1. "You formed my inward parts; You covered me in my mother's womb. I will praise You, for I am fearfully and wonderfully made; marvelous are Your works" (Psalm 139:13–14). What does this verse say about the way in which God created you? What does this say about the value that God sees in you?

....

....

....

....

....

....

2. "This is love, not that we loved God, but that He loved us and sent His Son to be the propitiation for our sins. Beloved, if God so loved us, we also ought to love one another" (1 John 4:10–11). Why does John command you to love *others*, rather than loving *yourself*? What does this suggest about a healthy self-image?

....

....

....

....

....

....

ACCEPTING RESPONSIBILITY FOR OUR SELF-IMAGE

Children draw much of their self-image from their parents. The ability of the parent to impart good self-worth and a positive self-image is based on his or her self-image and understanding of God's work in the child's life. If you have a poor self-image today, you must recognize that you have been taught that self-image. Your parents and others who had influence over you in your early childhood likely instilled it in you.

However, it is counterproductive to blame parents, teachers, and others for who you are today. In most cases, they didn't intend to impart a negative self-image. As an adult, you can make new choices. You can choose to believe the truth of God's Word—especially what God says about you as His beloved child. Forgive your parents for their failure to instill in you a good self-image, and move forward. Accept what your heavenly Father has to say about you.

Even if every parent was a master at instilling a positive self-image in his or her children, each child eventually faces the fact of the personal sin nature, which can be a major blow to self-image. Adam and Eve were created perfect—but then they sinned. As a result, they tried to hide from God and from each other. They also began to hide from themselves—they tried to justify their behavior to God. (Self-justification always involves some degree of hiding from the truth.) Adam and Eve found it extremely difficult to accept that they were no longer perfect.

Even people with healthy self-esteem must face this same reality. No one is perfect. All of us are in need of a Savior and the presence of the Holy Spirit to transform us into the likeness of Christ Jesus. Just as we must not blame our parents for our lack of a positive self-image, so we must not attempt to blame anyone else for the sinful nature that we inherited as our birthright. We must accept full responsibility for our self-image.

People with a good self-image are able to accept the good and bad in themselves. They are open to a relationship with God and with others. They express love freely and willingly, but always within the constraints of God's will. They expose their innermost feelings and ideas. They are confident of God's work in their lives and acknowledge that he is the source of all their abilities. They accommodate failures, learn from them, and move forward. Those who possess a positive self-image see that God—and future growth and development made possible by God—can more than make up for anything missing.

3. "Become complete. Be of good comfort, be of one mind, live in peace; and the God of love and peace will be with you" (2 Corinthians 13:11). According to this verse, what steps are required to "become complete"? Put each into your own words.

....

....

....

....

....

4. "Finally, brethren, whatever things are true, whatever things are noble, whatever things are just, whatever things are pure, whatever things are lovely, whatever things are of good report, if there is any virtue and if there is anything praiseworthy— meditate on these things" (Philippians 4:8). What are some examples in your life of things that are true, noble, just, pure, and lovely? How can you better focus on these things?

....

....

....

....

....

....

....

....

....

THE TRAPS OF GUILT, OVERACHIEVEMENT, AND CRITICISM

Your self-image gives you a sense of worth—a sense you are valuable to the kingdom of God. When you have a good self-image, you are willing to make yourself available to do God's work. Therefore, it is vital for you to maintain a good self-image that is rooted in Christ Jesus. For this reason, it is important to be aware of the following traps that can result when your self-image takes a "hit." These traps will keep you from being fully effective in serving the Lord.

First, the trap of guilt. Even after you have received God's forgiveness of your sin nature and have accepted Jesus as your Savior, you have the potential to commit sin. Indeed, you *do* sin, and with sin comes guilt. Unless you go to the Lord each time you have sinned and ask for His forgiveness, you are likely to develop a growing mountain of guilt. The more guilt you feel, the more you begin to question,

"How can God use me now?" Your self-image begins to disintegrate, and you can even become immobilized and ineffective in your Christian witness. So continually ask God's forgiveness for your sins. Don't accumulate guilt.

Second, the trap of overachievement. If you attempt to do it all, you run the risk of exhaustion. When you collapse in exhaustion and face the fact you haven't been able to do everything that you thought you could do, you are likely to become discouraged. Self-image takes a blow when you experience discouragement. The best way to stay out of the trap of overachievement is to ask the Lord every day what He desires for you to do during the day. Then, if you can't do it all, ask the Lord to help you readjust your priorities or manage your time better, or ask Him to enlarge your ability.

Live one day at a time. Learn to break down large tasks into smaller tasks, to set achievable goals for yourself at each stage of a large project, and to set aside time in your schedule for prayer, Bible reading, physical exercise, and relaxation. Get sufficient sleep. Above all, let the peace of God rule your life. The Lord will not ask you to do more than you can do.

Third, the trap of criticism. People who take to heart every bit of criticism have a great need for others to approve of them. The only approval that you need is that of the Lord Jesus. His approval is based on your desire to follow Him and to live according to His commandments. It is not based on your achievements, accomplishments, possessions, status, or level of income. If you diligently seek to love and serve the Lord, you have God's approval!

So don't listen to people who try to knock you down. Don't listen to people who criticize you no matter what you do. Such criticism is like a hammer against your self-image. It may be wise for you to take good counsel in improving certain skills, but it is unwise to listen to those who try to make you a better person according to *their* standards. The only standards that you need to be concerned about are ones in God's Word.

5. "If we confess our sins, He is faithful and just to forgive us our sins and to cleanse us from all unrighteousness" (1 John 1:9). Why is it important for a Christian to confess sins? What happens to our relationship with God otherwise? To our relationship with others? To our self-image?

6. "The righteous and the wise and their works are in the hand of God" (Ecclesiastes 9:1). If your works are "in the hand of God," what does that say about your accomplishments? About the goals that you don't achieve?

7. "Therefore let us pursue the things which make for peace and the things by which one may edify another" (Romans 14:19). What things "make for peace"? What things edify others? Give some practical examples.

....

....

....

....

....

....

THE TRAPS OF COMPARISON AND SCRIPTURAL ERROR

A fourth trap into which we can fall is that of comparison. This trap is similar to the trap of criticism. Some people continually gauge their performance by comparing themselves to others. They are much more concerned with being, having, owning, or achieving the best than in giving their best effort. Not everybody can be number one all the time. If you continually try to outdo all those around you, you are likely to suffer a major blow to your self-image each time you come in second best. The greater the failure, the greater the blow to your self-image.

Jesus Christ is established as our role model in the Bible. We are to grow up spiritually to become like Him. However, this does not mean that we will ever *be* Christ. He is the only perfect human who ever lived, and you are not going to experience His perfection in your humanity. Even so, the Holy Spirit is at work in you to transform you more and more into His likeness.

If you are a Christian yielded to the Holy Spirit, you are not the same person today that you were last year. And you won't be the same person this time next year that you are today. You are *growing* toward wholeness. So every time you are tempted to compare your accomplishments with someone else, concentrate on doing your best.

A final trap into which we can fall is that of scriptural error. Some people fall into this trap because they read the Bible incorrectly. Let me give you an example. In Luke 14:11, we read that Jesus says, "Whoever exalts himself will be humbled, and he who humbles himself will be exalted." Some people think this means that we should never receive a compliment or take credit for what we have done. To the contrary! Jesus made the statement in a specific setting. He told a parable to some people who were invited to a party and were vying for the best seats at the dinner table. He taught that the better approach was to take a lesser position of honor. In that context, the one who exalts himself is in a position to be humbled, while the one who humbles himself is in a position to be exalted.

This passage has nothing to do with self-image. Throughout the Bible, you are admonished to treat other people with kindness, respect, and honor. You are to serve others, give to others, and let others have their say and make their choices. But at no time are you told to deny the value the Lord places on you. There is a difference between being a kindhearted person and a person who has no regard for his talents, abilities, or stature in Christ.

Another passage that is often taught in error is Philippians 2:3: "Let nothing be done through selfish ambition or conceit, but in lowliness of mind let each esteem others better than himself." Some people think this means you should always give way to other people, saints and sinners alike. But Paul was speaking directly to the body of Christ. He was calling on the church to be "like-minded, having the same love, being of one accord, of one mind" in Christ Jesus (verse 2). He wanted God's people to get along in peace and harmony. Paul told them not to pursue their self-interests or think of themselves individually as better than the whole church. Rather, they should consider what was of benefit to the entire body of Christ: "Let each of you look out not only for his own interests, but also for the interests of others" (verse 4).

There is great balance in what Paul teaches. On the one hand, he calls on the church to be bold in dealing with sin, evil, and the assaults of the devil. On the other hand, he calls on the church members to be loving and generous with one another. We are to be alive in Christ, even as we are "dead" to all carnal influences. Paul carried this message to every church where he ministered. You can likewise be bold in denouncing evil and loving your brothers and sisters in Christ without any form of self-deprecation or self-hatred.

8. "Let your conduct be without covetousness; be content with such things as you have. For He Himself has said, 'I will never leave you nor forsake you'" (Hebrews 13:5). What does this verse say about comparing yourself to others?

....

....

....

....

....

....

9. "Aspire to lead a quiet life, to mind your own business, and to work with your own hands" (1 Thessalonians 4:11). How can striving to lead a quiet life, minding your own business, and working with your own hands help you to avoid the trap of comparison?

....

....

....

....

....

....

10. "Be diligent to present yourself approved to God, a worker who does not need to be ashamed, rightly dividing the word of truth" (2 Timothy 2:15). What does it mean to "rightly divide" God's Word? How is this done?

....

....

....

....

....

....

....

....

....

....

....

....

....

....

....

TODAY AND TOMORROW

Today: I must maintain a correct self-image based solely on the Word of God.

Tomorrow: I will ask the Lord to teach me about myself through His Word and His Spirit.

CLOSING PRAYER

. . . .

Lord, please help us today to stop dwelling on our past faults, failures, and weaknesses. Help us instead to concentrate on the victories we have witnessed in our lives and remember all of the times that You have answered our prayers. We want to live in the present and look to the future—to see what You see in us and what we are capable of becoming through Your guidance. Help us to realize that You accept us, love us, and value us as Your children.

NOTES AND
PRAYER REQUESTS

Use this space to write any key points, questions, or prayer requests from this week's study.

SEVEN KEYS TO EMOTIONAL WHOLENESS

Learning: How can I become emotionally whole?

Growing: What help does God provide in this process?

It is not enough merely to know the foundation for sound emotions or understand the relationship between a positive self-image and emotional well-being. You must also take the steps necessary to move from emotional weakness to emotional strength. There are at least seven major aspects of wholeness involved in seeking God's best for your emotional life. Think of these like having a ring of *keys*—all of which need to be inserted and turned simultaneously. These keys are habits that you must build into your life in an ongoing manner. As you do so, I have no doubt that you will become increasingly whole in your spirit and your emotions.

Give Your Heart to Christ and Saturate Yourself with Scripture

The first key is to *give your heart to Christ*. People who do not know Christ may claim they think the world of themselves . . . but they won't draw that conclusion if they are honest. Most unbelievers who state they are self-sufficient and don't need Christ are miserable people in crises. They are like beautiful flowering weeds with no strong root system. They have only themselves to rely on for strength, energy, enthusiasm, and creativity. Eventually, without the ability to draw on strength from the Holy Spirit, they come to the end of themselves.

Having a relationship with Christ Jesus resolves the issue of *feeling guilty*. Guilt is created when you have unforgiven sin, but when you ask for God's forgiveness, that guilt is washed away. It resolves the issue of *feeling unloved,* for when you turn to Christ, you accept that God loves you and desires to have an eternal relationship with you. It resolves the issue of *seeking revenge,* for once you accept God's free gift of salvation, you recognize God also wants to forgive others. It resolves the issue of *striving to earn favor with God,* for you realize God's gift of salvation to you is free. You can't earn it, buy it, or achieve it through good works. Any favor you have with God is solely on the basis of what Christ has done.

If you want to be emotionally whole today, give your life to Christ. Once you have accepted Christ Jesus as your personal Savior, you must then follow Him as your Lord. This daily following of Christ includes confessing sins—a daily cleansing of your spirit that is just as vital to your spiritual health as a daily rest is to your physical health. You affirm God's forgiveness for your sin nature and then seek forgiveness for the sins that you commit as you follow Christ.

The second key is to saturate yourself with Scripture. When you are forgiven, you have a clean slate before God, but it isn't enough to just have a clean slate. You need to ask the Lord to write His truth on the slate of your heart. You acquire God's truth about virtually every situation by reading His Word and saturating yourself with His opinion. In the area of emotional health, this means saturating yourself with God's opinion about you.

In the Bible, you discover that you are *a child of God* (see Galatians 3:26–27; 1 John 5:1–2), that you are *accepted totally and completely by God* (see Acts 10:34–35; Ephesians 1:3,6), and that you are *an heir of the Father through Christ Jesus* (see Galatians 3:29; Titus 3:7). Many other descriptions of God's people appear in the Scriptures. You may want to start a list or circle them as you read your Bible daily. If you are born again into Christ Jesus, all of these descriptions about the children of God apply to *you*. Take them as part of your profile.

1. "All that the Father gives Me will come to Me, and the one who comes to Me I will by no means cast out" (John 6:37). How has accepting God's gift of salvation resolved issues in your life of experiencing guilt, feeling unloved, seeking revenge, or striving to earn the favor and respect of others? What has God done to change your emotional life?

   ....

   ....

   ....

   ....

   ....

2. "For you are all sons of God through faith in Christ Jesus. For as many of you as were baptized into Christ have put on Christ" (Galatians 3:26–27). What does it mean to "put on Christ"? How is this done, in practical terms?

   ....

   ....

   ....

   ....

   ....

SECURE GOD'S HEALING FOR YOUR FAULTS AND STOP BARTERING

The third key is to secure God's healing for your faults. We all have some-thing about ourselves we don't like. We all have a tendency to concen-trate more on the flaws than on the strengths. Some things in life cannot be changed. For example, you can't change the family into which you were born or your physical stature. Likewise, certain phys-ical weaknesses or disabilities cannot be changed. When you face these unchangeable things about yourself, you are wise to accept the way that God made you. To do anything else is counterproductive.

Some things in life are unchangeable because of the world in which you live. For example, you may not be able to alter the fact that your parents are divorced. But you can pray that the Lord will bring about healing in your life and in the lives of your loved ones. However, there are elements of your personality that *can* be changed. For exam-ple, you may think that you are jealous by nature. But let me assure you, envy is an acquired trait. You can ask the Lord to heal you of your jealousy and to help you to trust Him and others.

How do you become healed? First, you identify the character trait that you know is displeasing to the Lord and ask Him to forgive you for allowing this trait to develop. Second, you ask Him to heal you of this tendency. Third, you give Him permission to do whatever He needs to do in your life to make you whole. Fourth, you have faith that God is at work in your life and that He will make you whole in His timing and according to His methods. God is merciful. He for-gives, heals, and enters any area that you open up to Him.

The fourth key is to stop bartering with God. Maybe you think that if you just work hard enough and do enough good in your life, God will approve of you. If so, you are attempting to *barter* good works for God's acceptance. You may have difficulty accepting the mercy of God because you have never fully received His love. Or you may be so accustomed to the give-and-take, buy-and-sell nature of our culture that you assume you can deal with God the same way: "You do this for me and I'll do this for You." God doesn't operate according to that human principle.

God's principle is one of total acceptance of you when you ask for His forgiveness and do His will. If He desires to change something in your life, His chastisement is patient and kind (never beyond your ability to bear), and His love is constant (never withheld or removed). You can't barter your way around God's will, so stop trying. Trust God. Ask Him for what you desire, and then trust Him to answer your prayer according to His wisdom and infinite provision.

3. "Now may the God of peace Himself sanctify you completely; and may your whole spirit, soul, and body be preserved blameless at the coming of our Lord Jesus Christ. He who calls you is faithful, who also will do it" (1 Thessalonians 5:23–24). What part does God play in your sanctification? What part do you play?

....

....

....

....

....

4. "Therefore do not worry, saying, 'What shall we eat?' or 'What shall we drink?' or 'What shall we wear?' . . . For your heavenly Father knows that you need all these things. But seek first the kingdom of God and His righteousness, and all these things shall be added to you" (Matthew 6:31–33). How does worry influence your emotional life? What should you be seeking instead?

....

....

....

....

....

SHARE YOURSELF WITH OTHERS AND DON'T DWELL ON THE PAST

The fifth key is to share yourself with others. Too much introspection into your problems and weaknesses can cause you to become ingrown. If you've ever had an ingrown toenail, you know how just a small ingrown element of your physical body can cause pain. This same principle applies to your spiritual and emotional life. You can turn inward and over time cause great damage to yourself—all in the name of trying to know yourself or fix your problems.

The best cure for many emotional difficulties is to turn outward and start giving to others. Every person has something to give, even if it's only a smile, a kind word, or a pat on the shoulder in a time of need. Sometimes just your presence can be a gift to someone. The happiest people I know are those who have wide-open hearts and who give generously to others. Such individuals are secure in God's love.

Give without expecting anything in return. God will see your heart and what you do and reward you accordingly. Trust Him to take care of you. As you do this, you open up yourself. This open stance before God and other people is important to emotional health. It is only as you open yourself that you learn to trust. Being able to trust is vital to your ability to receive God's forgiveness and healing and to believing that God will supply your needs.

The sixth key is to stop dwelling on your past. Part of receiving God's forgiveness is forgiving yourself. Once God has forgiven you, you have no claim to your past sins, failures, or weaknesses. You are a new creature in Christ Jesus! Each time you dwell on your past failures, you are closing your heart and mind to the blessing that God has for you. So force yourself to think instead of the many ways that God has helped you and blessed you. Any time you find yourself reflecting on past failures, remind yourself that God has delivered you from sin. Then turn your mind to the positive things that God has done for you, in you, and through you. Start praising Him for His goodness.

5. "Heal the sick, cleanse the lepers, raise the dead, cast out demons. Freely you have received, freely give" (Matthew 10:8). What have you received freely from God? What can you give to others?

....

....

....

....

....

....

6. "You who love the LORD, hate evil! He preserves the souls of His saints; He delivers them out of the hand of the wicked" (Psalm 97:10). What is the difference between hating your own sin and refusing to forgive yourself for it? How can a correct balance bring emotional healing?

....

....

....

....

....

....

ASK THE HOLY SPIRIT FOR HELP

The seventh key is to ask the Holy Spirit for help. The Holy Spirit is imparted to you when you place your trust in Jesus Christ. The ministry of the Holy Spirit is to give you daily guidance and counsel, to help you walk in the ways of the Lord, and to enable you to make wise choices. Ask for the help of the Holy Spirit on a daily basis. Ask Him to guard you from evil and to guide you into righteousness. Give Him charge over your schedule and your daily appointments. Trust Him to bring you to people in need so that you might minister to them, and to help you in the form that is best for you.

7. "I will pray the Father, and He will give you another Helper, that He may abide with you forever—the Spirit of truth, whom the world cannot receive, because it neither sees Him nor knows Him" (John 14:16–17). What sort of help does the Holy Spirit offer to Christians? When have you experienced His help?

....

....

....

....

....

....

8. Why do you think that Jesus refers to the Holy Spirit as "the Spirit of truth"? Why is truth important to emotional health?

....

....

....

....

....

....

9. "Having been justified by His grace we should become heirs according to the hope of eternal life" (Titus 3:7). What is the inheritance promised to Christians? How does this inheritance affect you emotionally?

....

....

....

....

....

....

10. What is "the hope of eternal life"? How should the hope of *eternal* life influence your emotional responses to your *daily* life?

....

....

....

....

....

TODAY AND TOMORROW

Today: My relationship with God is the most important element in becoming emotionally whole.

Tomorrow: I will immerse myself in God's Word and submit myself to His Holy Spirit this week.

CLOSING PRAYER

Father, we pray You will continue the process You began in bringing our emotions under Your control. We give our hearts to you—completely and without holding anything back. We resolve to saturate ourselves with Scripture so we can see ourselves the way You see us. We seek Your healing for our false beliefs and choose to stop trying to "bargain" with You—knowing there is nothing we can do to earn Your approval. We choose to share our lives with others and not dwell on the past. Finally, we ask the Holy Spirit to empower us to help us make wise and healthy choices—especially as it relates to emotions we express in the presence of others.

NOTES AND
PRAYER REQUESTS

Use this space to write any key points, questions, or prayer requests from this week's study.

LESSON 6

The Ache of Anxiety

IN THIS LESSON

Learning: Where does my deep anxiety come from?

Growing: How can I tap into God's power to remove it?

Our world is filled with anxious people. People are anxious about the future, unseen dangers, personal status, their health, their relationships, and their ability to succeed in life. Many are anxious about the state of their souls and whether they are in right standing with God. Even Christians have these concerns.

In the Sermon on the Mount, Jesus dealt with the topic of anxiety when He said, "Do not worry, saying, 'What shall we eat?' or 'What shall we drink?' or 'What shall we wear?' For after all these things the Gentiles seek. For your heavenly Father knows that you need all these things. But seek first the kingdom of God and His righteousness, and all these things shall be added to you. Therefore do not worry about tomorrow, for tomorrow will worry about its own things. Sufficient for the day is its own trouble" (Matthew 6:31–34).

69

The concept of anxiety is found throughout the New Testament. In Greek, the word *merimna* is generally used—it means "to take thought." Issues such as the ones that Jesus raised in this passage aren't even to enter our minds . . . but if they do, we are to give them no lodging. We are not to give them a second thought, for they are not worth thinking about. Yet how many of us spend anxious moments pondering what we will eat, drink, or wear, or how we will meet other daily practical needs in our lives? After all, food, drink, and clothing are some of our most basic needs. This is exactly the point that Jesus is making: God knows our basic needs. He is capable of meeting them . . . and He *desires* to meet them.

1. What did Jesus mean when He said, "Sufficient for the day is its own trouble"? How does tackling today's problems and setting future goals differ from worrying about tomorrow?

   ....

   ....

   ....

   ....

   ....

2. What things do you tend to worry about? How do Jesus' words apply to *your* situation?

   ....

   ....

   ....

   ....

   ....

THE ATTITUDE OF ANXIETY

An attitude of anxiety goes beyond mere moments of feeling anxious from time to time. Anxiety involves being pulled in two directions—it is an inner war. You are faced with choices about which direction to go or which consequence might occur. You have a divided mind and a degree of fear that you might make the wrong choice. Anxiety is rarely a product of your environment. Certain circumstances don't automatically result in anxiety. What causes anxiety in some people doesn't affect other people at all. To a great extent, anxiety is a matter of *attitude*.

Consider the issue of public speaking. Some people delight in it. Others cringe at the very thought—their palms get clammy, their heads spin, they feel nauseous, and they start looking for an exit door. Anxiety takes over. Public speaking in itself does not produce anxiety. Rather, the consequences related to public speaking create anxiety. Often, people try to blame events, people, or situations for their anxiety. But anxiety lies within. It is an emotional response to a situation that can typically be controlled through the exercise of the will.

In an earlier lesson, I mentioned that every emotional response to life has a positive and negative side. On the positive side, a little anxiety can motivate us to action. If we forget to set the alarm and are on the verge of being late to work, the anxiety can cause us to hurry a little to get to work on time. On the negative side, however, is the possibility of deep-seated despair. When anxiety is allowed to develop into a pattern in our lives, it can be devastating.

3. What situations (such as public speaking) are most likely to cause you anxiety? What about that particular situation makes you anxious?

4. How might you decrease your anxiety in such situations by changing your thinking?

....

....

....

....

....

THREE CAUSES OF ANXIETY

There are at least three major causes of anxiety. *First, you perceive that you won't be able to meet your needs.* When Jesus preached the Sermon on the Mount around AD 30, the people in Judea were living in poverty. The Romans had drained the wealth of the land through taxation and acquisition. There were no social welfare programs as we know them today. People were consumed with earning enough just to meet the basic needs of food, shelter, and clothing. Today, this cause of anxiety might be worry about paying the bills, finding a job, or providing sufficiently for families. The causes of anxiety at this level are real, practical, and material.

Second, you set standards that can't be met, resulting in repeated failure and frustration. Much of this anxiety is rooted in intangible expectations, dreams, or goals. Sometimes unrealistic standards are set by others—such as supervisors, parents, or spouses—but when that is the case, the response is usually not anxiety as much as anger or resentment. It is only when you internalize the unrealistic expectations that anxiety takes over. Some people set standards for themselves that are far higher than those set by God! They expect absolute perfection in everything they do as well as everything that others do.

Third, you have unresolved hostility. When you feel anger, bitterness, or resentment over a period of time, you will feel a constant agitation or irritation in your spirit. Again, this cause of anxiety is *internal*. Anxiety that is rooted in high expectations or unresolved hostility is just as real as anxiety about basic material needs. The anxiety is real, it is just as damaging, and it has the same hallmarks.

5. When have you experienced anxiety in each of these three areas? What caused the anxiety?

....

....

....

....

....

6. How is anxiety in each of these areas increased by your thoughts and attitudes? How much is caused by external factors?

....

....

....

....

....

THE SIGNS OF ANXIETY

In Proverbs 12:25, we read, "Anxiety in the heart of man causes depression." In the King James Version, this verse reads, "Heaviness in the heart of man maketh it stoop." Anxiety pulls us down. The symptoms associated with anxiety vary from person to person, but they generally involve one or more of these characteristics: forgetfulness, inability to concentrate, irritability, inability to cope with small problems, vacillation in making decisions, misjudging other people, feeling persecuted, procrastination, and gnawing dissatisfaction.

These symptoms have dire consequences if they continue unchecked. Some consequences include: a feeling of drudgery about life, especially toward work and tasks; a loss of excitement and enthusiasm; a loss of productivity, creativity, and energy; and damage to the physical body. In other words, nothing good comes from anxiety! Jesus referred to some of the negative results of anxiety in a parable that He told:

> When anyone hears the word of the kingdom, and does not understand it, then the wicked one comes and snatches away what was sown in his heart. This is he who received seed by the wayside. But he who received the seed on stony places, this is he who hears the word and immediately receives it with joy; yet he has no root in himself, but endures only for a while. For when tribulation or persecution arises because of the word, immediately he stumbles. Now he who received seed among the thorns is he who hears the word, and the cares of this world and the deceitfulness of riches choke the word, and he becomes unfruitful. But he who received seed on the good ground is he who hears the word and understands it, who indeed bears fruit and produces: some a hundredfold, some sixty, some thirty (Matthew 13:19–23).

The "cares of this world" choke off the productivity of a good seed sown in your life. When you allow yourself to become enveloped in anxiety, you become almost immune to any positive word, expression of faith, or insight from God. If you are anxious, you are so overwhelmed in looking at your problems that you can't think clearly about the solutions. When that happens, the Word has little impact in your life, which eliminates the very thing that can build faith and counteract anxiety. The spiral is downward.

Have you ever tried to read your Bible, only to find that you've gone through several verses and don't have any recollection of what you have read? Chances are that anxiety was at work. You were seeing the words with your eyes, but other cares and concerns kept you from taking in the words. Note that Jesus taught this parable about the *kingdom of God*. He said that the "wicked one" snatches away some of the seed planted in our lives. But that isn't the case with anxiety. You have a tremendous measure of control over your anxiety.

If you have a loss of interest in life, consider whether you have nurtured an attitude of anxiety. If so, it is up to you to take action to break the hold that worry has over you. God will help you, but you must face what you have allowed to develop in your life and take action to counteract your response of worry and anxiety.

7. What do thorns and weeds do to plants in a garden? How is this a picture of worry and anxiety in your life?

....
....
....
....
....

8. In what ways do we actually do the work of the devil when we allow anxiety to remain in our hearts? What is the solution to this pattern?

....
....
....
....
....

GOD'S ANSWER TO ANXIETY

There are no easy solutions if you have allowed anxiety to take root in your life. You literally need to take hold of your mind and corral it, refusing to let anxiety reign. So-called "solutions" such as turning to drugs and alcohol, going on wanton shopping sprees, or even making major life changes will not alleviate deep feelings of anxiety.

All of these behaviors merely seek to substitute something for anxiety other than the peace of Jesus Christ.

These compulsive behaviors only add to the problem. They may mask anxiety for a while, but it continues to brew and build. Eventually, you *must* deal with anxiety or face a serious breakdown. When that time comes—and it inevitably comes—you face a mountain of anxiety and the problem of a possible addiction to the drugs, alcohol, or behavior sought as a solution.

You must deal with emotional anxiety at its source: *a failure to trust God*. At the foundation of anxiety is the mistaken belief that either God can't take care of the situation, or He won't—and either way, you lose because God doesn't act. The only lasting and healing solution for an attitude of anxiety is to place your trust in God.

This begins by turning your heart over to God. If your relationship is wrong with God, you can't be right in yourself. If you are cut off from God's peace, you ultimately can have no peace. If you are a Christian, you must come to God and confess that you have failed to trust Him completely. Ask Him to forgive you for trying to live your life according to your own plans, abilities, agendas, and talents. Receive His forgiveness, and ask the Holy Spirit to help you trust God with your whole heart, mind, and soul. You may need to confess this to God many times in your life. The process is one of trusting Him more and more.

Second, tell God about how you feel. Something beneficial comes from admitting to God the anxiety that you feel. In Philippians 4:6, Paul admonishes you to "be anxious for nothing." This phrase is followed by a call to prayer: "But in everything by prayer and supplication, with thanksgiving, let your requests be made known to God." The antidote for moments of anxiety is *prayer*. Supplication refers to making petitions before God, asking Him specifically for what you desire. You are to accompany the prayer and supplication with thanksgiving—giving thanks even before you receive God's provision for the answer that you know is on the way!

You can know God's answer is coming because He is faithful to His Word. He loves you as His child and provides for you. In giving thanks, you are giving voice to the trust that you are placing in God to love you and care for you. What is the result of this kind of prayer? Paul states, "The peace of God, which surpasses all understanding, will guard your [heart] and [mind] through Christ Jesus" (verse 7). Through prayer, you *become* anxious for nothing and have the peace of God, instead of worry and its related frustrations and damaging effects.

Third, turn the anxiety-causing problem over to God. After you have prayed about your anxiety and the problem that gave rise to it, leave your problem with God. As Peter wrote, "Casting all your care upon Him, for He cares for you" (1 Peter 5:7). Trusting God to solve your problem or meet your need means that you give the problem to God *completely.* Give Him *all* of your concern, anxiety, worry.

Finally, turn your mind to the blessings of God. Choose to think about something other than your problem. Dwell on answers, hopes, dreams, new opportunities, and good things of all types. Recall the many promises of God to you as His child. Search through your Bible and underscore passages of Scripture that speak of God's blessings, provision, and peace. (Use a concordance to find as many verses as you can.)

9. "He who dwells in the secret place of the Most High Shall abide under the shadow of the Almighty. I will say of the LORD, 'He is my refuge and my fortress; My God, in Him I will trust'" (Psalm 91:1–2). How can a fortress keep a person safe from external dangers? In what ways is God like this to His children?

10. "Peace I leave with you, My peace I give to you; not as the world gives do I give to you. Let not your heart be troubled, neither let it be afraid" (John 14:27). Why do you think Jesus commanded us not to let our hearts be troubled or afraid? How are fear and trouble under our control?

....

....

....

....

....

....

....

....

....

....

....

FOCUS ON GOD

Paul advised the Philippians to be anxious for nothing, and then told them to pray and give supplication to God with thanksgiving, promising them God's peace. His very next words encouraged the Philippians to meditate on praiseworthy things (see Philippians 4:8.) This advice is the same for you today! So much of the world is steeped in bad news. How important it is for you to be steeped in even greater quantities of good news.

Direct your reading, your media watching, and your conversations to what is *good*. After all, a mind concentrating on God's presence has no time to dwell on problems, while a mind concentrating on God's goodness only results in emotions of anticipation, hope, faith, and joy. Such an emotional state is the very opposite of anxiety and worry. So focus on praiseworthy things. Discuss with others how the Lord is working in your life—how He is healing you, strengthening you, and bringing you to a higher plane in your spiritual life. Share with others the testimonies of people you know. Build up your faith and the faith of others.

When you have a praiseworthy, optimistic, faith-filled approach to life, anxiety-causing situations will not affect you nearly as much as when you have a negative, God-has-forgotten-me attitude. Your best approach to prevent anxiety is to concentrate on the praiseworthy and to voice your praise to God. Make abundant praise a daily part of your prayer life.

TODAY AND TOMORROW

Today: My thought life is vital to fighting anxiety.

Tomorrow: I will immerse myself in Scripture, praise, and prayer this week.

CLOSING PRAYER

Jesus, thank You for allowing us to see that You experienced the range of emotions we face today. When we think about You in the Garden of Gethsemane, crying with perspiration that looked like drops of blood . . . we understand the great anxiety You faced. Your Word provides a comfort to us in knowing that You can relate to how we feel. We will never experience anything that You did not already face—You understand us because You were one of us. Thank You for Your willingness to become human enough to feel what we feel.

NOTES AND
PRAYER REQUESTS

Use this space to write any key points, questions, or prayer requests from this week's study.

LESSON 7

THE GRIP OF FEAR

IN THIS LESSON

Learning: When is fear healthy, and when is it unhealthy?

Growing: How should I respond to both types of fear?

Fear is one of the most potent emotions we can feel. It is our number one natural defense against all things that are harmful to us. Everybody is afraid of *something*. I defy any person to come face-to-face with a shark, a coiled rattlesnake, or a grizzly bear and *not* feel fear.

The disciples of Jesus certainly experienced fear. On one occasion, they were on the Sea of Galilee when a storm arose. Matthew tells us, "But the boat was now in the middle of the sea, tossed by the waves, for the wind was contrary. Now in the fourth watch of the night Jesus went to them, walking on the sea. And when the disciples saw Him walking on the sea, they were troubled, saying, 'It is a ghost!' And they cried out for fear. But immediately Jesus spoke to them saying, 'Be of good cheer! It is I; do not be afraid'" (Matthew 14:24–27).

The disciples were afraid of what they didn't perceive fully . . . and they were afraid of what they thought had the potential to hurt or destroy them. That is the nature of fear: we fear what we don't know, and we fear what we think will hurt us.

Types of Healthy Fear

Fear comes in two varieties: positive fear (which is good and related to health and safety), and negative fear (which is damaging). We *should* fear some things. For instance, *we should have a healthy fear of the Lord.* Think of this type of fear as reverence or awe. When we encounter the Lord, we come into the presence of the King of the universe. The Lord has the power to destroy, but the fear that we feel about the judgment of God must be balanced with our awe that God is all-loving and ever merciful to us as His children. Our fear of God is a healthy fear to have. It is the awe of humble children before an awesome Father.

Adam and Eve had a fear of God after they sinned in the Garden of Eden, and they hid. They then attempted to justify their actions and placed the blame on someone else. Ever since then, men and women have been responding the same—by attempting to hide from God or trying to convince ourselves that He doesn't exist. The only solution to this problem is to face God and to admit that we are afraid, that we've been running, and that we have sinned. We come to the Father and own up to our sin, accept what Jesus did on the cross in providing a sacrifice for it, and then ask God for forgiveness.

In addition to having a fear of the Lord, *we should also have a healthy fear of sin.* Sin has the power to destroy our lives, causing great damage to us today and even affecting our eternal destiny. When we fear sin, we fear the consequences of sin . . . which the Bible reveals are deadly. Many people dismiss the nature of sin. In part, they do this because we all sin, and they have a false notion that if everybody is doing it, it must be all right.

These people deny the power of sin because they *hope* that the Lord God might overlook it, and thus the sin will have no consequences in their lives. But this line of thinking is completely wrong. God never overlooks sin, and it never goes unpunished. God's Word clearly defines the nature of sin and the nature of righteousness, and it declares the consequence for unrepented, unforgiven sin is ultimately eternal death for unbelievers.

We should also have a healthy fear of Satan, the enemy of our soul. Jesus said that Satan is a thief who has the power to steal, kill, and destroy (see John 10:10). He is a formidable enemy, stronger than we are but weaker than Christ Jesus. Only as we live in right standing with the Father (through the redemptive work of Christ), live out the will of God, and use the name of Jesus will we have authority to resist the devil and overcome him.

Too many Christians speak lightly of the devil. They treat him as if he is a human enemy that can be easily defeated. The Scriptures give us a much different portrayal of the enemy of our souls. They tell us that Satan is the father of all lies and deception, the master manipulator, the archenemy of God, and the one who continually seeks to devour us as a roaring lion.

In addition to a healthy fear of God, sin, and the devil, there are other healthy fears. Parents attempt to teach their children a fear of touching a hot stove, running out in the street, and talking to strangers. We seem to be born with a healthy fear of sudden loud noises and of falling. It is natural to feel a moment of fear when we hear an unusual sound outside the home or hear the sirens warning of a storm. As stated earlier, such fears motivate us to act.

What we need to do in the face of such fears is to act in a positive manner. Our fear of a hot stove is healthy if we respond by not touching a hot stove. Our fear of a warning siren is healthy if we respond by seeking shelter. And our fear of sin is healthy if we respond by seeking forgiveness and repenting (making a change in the will to not commit the sin again).

1. "They heard the sound of the LORD God walking in the garden in the cool of the day, and Adam and his wife hid themselves from the presence of the LORD God among the trees of the garden. Then the LORD God called to Adam and said to him, 'Where are you?' So he said, 'I heard Your voice in the garden, and I was afraid because I was naked; and I hid myself'" (Genesis 3:8–10). Notice the repetition of the word "I" in Adam's response. What does this suggest about fear? How did Adam respond to his fear?

....

....

....

....

....

2. "The fear of the LORD is the beginning of knowledge, but fools despise wisdom and instruction" (Proverbs 1:7). How does the fear described in this verse differ from Adam's fear? How does this represent a healthy kind of fear?

....

....

....

....

....

3. "Be sober, be vigilant; because your adversary the devil walks about like a roaring lion, seeking whom he may devour" (1 Peter 5:8). What does it mean to be "sober" and "vigilant" against sin?

....

....

....

....

....

Types of Unhealthy Fear

When we respond in a negative manner, our fear is unhealthy. Negative responses include being paralyzed by fear (unable to move or take evasive action), being frazzled by fear (moving in too many directions at once, or running in circles), and being overwhelmed by fear (so that we respond by hiding from all of life). The result of such negative responses to fear is that we don't act in a way that brings us relief from fear. In failing to move or act, we place ourselves in continued danger and, therefore, in continued fear.

Healthy fear is for our protection, both in the natural and spiritual realms. However, unhealthy fear can be devastating. As Paul warned Timothy: "I remind you to stir up the gift of God which is in you through the laying on of my hands. For God has not given us a spirit of fear, but of power and of love and of a sound mind" (2 Timothy 1:6-7). An unhealthy fear diminishes us spiritually, making us fail to give a bold witness of Christ, take risks in launching new ministries, respond fully to God's love, and grow in our faith.

Fear demoralizes us and robs us of hope. When we no longer have hope, we give in to despair, depression, and dejection. We lose an awareness of possibility, dreams, and goals.

4. What healthy fears did you learn as a child? How did you learn them? When have you responded to a threat in your life with an unhealthy fear?

....

....

....

....

....

5. "But I want you to know, brethren, that the things which happened to me have actually turned out for the furtherance of the

gospel, so that it has become evident to the whole palace guard, and to all the rest, that my chains are in Christ; and most of the brethren in the Lord, having become confident by my chains, are much more bold to speak the word without fear" (Philippians 1:12–14). Paul wrote these words when he was in prison for his faith. How did he respond to a fearful situation?

....

....

....

....

....

BASIC FEARS THAT WE FACE

Every person faces certain fears that have been present throughout the ages. These include fears such as *poverty*—the fear of not having enough material substance. We fear losing our sources of income, bill collectors, creditors, and the possibility of bankruptcy. *Death* and *ill heath* are other basic fears. We fear the unknown "beyond" and worry about becoming incapacitated. We fear pain and suffering.

Loss of love is another basic fear. We worry about the possibility of divorce, estrangement, and the loss of contact with loved ones. We fear parents dying and children leaving home. We fear those who might draw our loved ones away from us. We may fear *old age,* and becoming isolated and lonely. We fear losing our capacity to work and an increasing inability to do those things that we did when we were young. We also fear *criticism.* We worry about what others will think of us and say about us.

We can choose to respond positively to each of these basic fears. For example, we can do many things to keep ourselves healthy as we age. We can build retirement or savings plans to avert future poverty. We can stay interested in life, continue to learn new things, and work to strengthen friendships and family ties. We can also inform ourselves more fully in areas where a lack of knowledge contributes to fear.

Or we can respond negatively to our fears. When we do, we nearly always visualize *potential* negative consequences, or things that *might* happen that are not inevitable. Some of what we imagine is an illusion. Even so, our bodies tend to react to negative, fearful imaginations as if what we are imagining is real. This is especially true in the area of criticism. Many people dread encounters with certain people. As a result, they refuse to go to certain places or engage in certain activities that might be beneficial for them because they fear being ridiculed or otherwise criticized. The people that they fear have a "hold" on their lives.

Negative fears and an unhealthy response to fear can result in a *spirit of fear*. This spirit of timidity keeps us from taking risks of love. It keeps us from reaching out to others, from revealing our innermost thoughts and feelings, from developing deep, satisfying relationships. Fear that is not healed by God becomes a pervasive emotional response to all of life, whether meeting new people, pursuing new opportunities, facing challenges, or standing up against evil. When a spirit of fear takes hold, we are unable to help ourselves. We need loving friends to intercede in prayer on our behalf. We always need wise counsel from a godly person.

6. "The fear of man brings a snare, but whoever trusts in the LORD shall be safe" (Proverbs 29:25). Which people have brought fear into your life? How did you respond to that fear?

....

....

....

....

....

....

....

7. Imagine the Lord walking beside you as you encountered one of those people. How would your response be different?

....

....

....

....

....

8. "Let your conduct be without covetousness; be content with such things as you have. For He Himself has said, 'I will never leave you nor forsake you.' So we may boldly say: 'The Lord is my helper; I will not fear. What can man do to me?'" (Hebrews 13:5–6). What part does covetousness play in anxiety? What forms of fear might be rooted in it?

....

....

....

....

....

....

RESPONSE TO THE GRIP OF FEAR

Remember Paul's words to Timothy: "God has not given us a spirit of fear, but of power and of love and of a sound mind" (2 Timothy 1:7). Your response to every person or situation that you fear is to rely on God's power, God's love, and God's mind.

First, ask for God's help. When you are struck with fear, your first response should be to ask for God's help. Avail yourself of the power of God. At the beginning of this lesson, we read how Jesus walked on the sea to His disciples. Peter heard the Lord say, "Be of good cheer!" and he said, "Lord, if it is You, command me to come to You on the water" (Matthew 14:28).

Jesus commanded Peter to come to Him on the waves. So Peter stepped out of the boat and walked on the water toward Jesus. But when he looked around and saw that the wind and the waves were fierce, he became afraid and started to sink. It was then that Peter called out, "Lord, save me!" (verse 30). This was the right response—to ask for God's help. "Immediately Jesus stretched out His hand and caught him" (verse 31). Likewise, your first response when you feel fear should be to say, "Lord, save me!"

Second, ask for God's love to fill your heart. Love is a potent antidote for fear. I recall the first time I preached in my home church. I had a "fear attack." The people knew me, and I felt they expected more from me than a group of strangers might expect. So I read the words of the Lord to Joshua in Joshua 1:5–9, and then I turned my focus on the people of my home church. I was quickly overwhelmed by how much I loved them. The more I thought about how much I loved them and how they had loved me through the years, the more my fear evaporated. When I stood in the pulpit, the fear completely drained out of me, and I felt full of God's love, the power of His anointing, and the desire to preach God's Word.

John had a great deal to say about God's love—both in his gospel and in his letters to the church. As we read in 1 John 4:17–18, "Love has been perfected among us in this: that we may have boldness in the day of judgment; because as He is, so are we in this world. There is no fear in love; but perfect love casts out fear, because fear involves torment. But he who fears has not been made perfect in love." So ask your heavenly Father to impart to you more of Christ's love and to take away any torment that you feel. Let the perfect love of Jesus Christ flood your soul. As you do, fear will lose its grip on you.

Third, ask God to give you a sound mind filled with God's Word. The basis for a sound mind is the Word of God. The more you know of God's promises to you, and the more you live according to His commandments, the greater your strength to withstand fear. Memorize Isaiah 41:10: "Fear not, for I am with you; be not dismayed, for

I am your God. I will strengthen you, yes, I will help you, I will uphold you with My righteous right hand." You can use this verse to speak to the source of your fear, just as Jesus quoted Scripture to the devil during His time of temptation in the wilderness (see Luke 4:1–13).

When you are gripped by fear, turn your gaze on God, redirect your heart to love, speak to your fear from the Word of God, and then respond boldly to the situation that caused your fear. The Lord wants you to "be strong and of good courage."

9. "Only be strong and very courageous, that you may observe to do according to all the law which Moses My servant commanded you; do not turn from it to the right hand or to the left, that you may prosper wherever you go" (Joshua 1:7). Why did God instruct Joshua to be strong and courageous? What purpose did He have?

....

....

....

....

....

10. "This Book of the Law shall not depart from your mouth, but you shall meditate in it day and night, that you may observe to do according to all that is written in it. . . . Be strong and of good courage; do not be afraid, nor be dismayed, for the Lord your God is with you wherever you go" (Joshua 1:8–9). What instruction did God give to Joshua? What promise did He make to bolster Joshua's confidence?

....

....

....

....

....

....

TODAY AND TOMORROW

Today: A healthy response to fear always drives me closer to God.

Tomorrow: I will spend time this week memorizing Isaiah 41:10.

CLOSING PRAYER

Heavenly Father, please help us to keep our eyes fixed on You. We know that You are using the trials in our lives—challenges that can make us fearful— to teach us something. While it feels as if we are going down fast, we know that You are always in control. You know exactly where we are in the wind and the waves . . . and Your purpose for having us face this situation. Help us not to panic but to put our faith in You. We are available to learn everything You wish to teach us. We choose to trust in You today and not submit to the feelings of fear.

NOTES AND
PRAYER REQUESTS

. . . .

Use this space to write any key points, questions, or prayer requests
from this week's study.

THE GRINDSTONE
OF GUILT

IN THIS LESSON

Learning: If I have confessed my sin, why do
I still feel guilty?

Growing: How can I gain something good from
my bad experiences?

Guilt is like a giant weight on the heart and mind that slowly grinds down a person's enthusiasm, hope, and joy. It represents a serious detriment to the kingdom of God when it manifests itself in feelings of unworthiness to be used by God in various areas of witness, outreach, or ministry, or to receive His abundant blessings.

In such cases, the memories of past mistakes come flooding back, along with a built-in guilt message, "And because of that, God can't use you," or, "Because of your failure, God can't bless you." Guilt never allows you to forget what you once did. Christians in many denominations have built a case against themselves that keeps them from receiving all that God has for them and from doing all that God wants them to do.

Guilt is the fear of being found out and being punished for a sin or mistake. We all experience guilt at some point because we all sin and make mistakes. The question is not *whether* we experience guilt, but *how* we will deal with it when it comes.

THE REMEDY FOR GUILT

A sense of guilt about one's sinful nature is often a factor in a person coming to Christ. With this in mind, let me remind you of several things about God's forgiveness as we deal with this issue of guilt. *First, forgiveness has already been provided by God prior to us asking for it.* Jesus died on the cross as the perfect, complete, and only sacrifice necessary to free us from sin.

Second, we don't need to plead for forgiveness or try to impress on God that we are worthy to be forgiven. We need to accept and *receive* what God has provided through Christ. When we ask for forgiveness, God freely and unconditionally grants it (see 1 John 1:9). Furthermore, we can't do anything that will impress God to forgive us on the basis of our merits. His sinless Son has already died on our behalf. What more could we possibly do?

Third, we need to remember that God's forgiveness is not automatic. We must accept it. We do this by coming to God in humility, admitting that we are sinners in need of forgiveness. We acknowledge that Jesus Christ died on our behalf and believe that what He did provides the means of forgiveness. Some people call this an act of confession. You may question why you need to do this if God has already forgiven you. The purpose is that you might know in your heart that you are forgiven and then experience the cleansing power of forgiveness.

The aftermath of receiving God's forgiveness is to repent for our past sins, make a choice to follow in the footsteps of Jesus, and live according to God's commandments. The ability to follow through on this new commitment comes from the indwelling power of the Holy Spirit, who joins with our spirit at the time we receive God's forgiveness. Thus, God forgives us from past sins and enables us to not sin in the future (see 1 John 5:18).

An unregenerate sin nature produces a *state* of guilt. Those who have never received God's forgiveness have a perpetual underlying guilt they can never escape. They may harden their hearts to the point that it *seems* they no longer feel guilty for their sin, but deep inside, they know they are estranged from God and feel their sin and its related guilt. Sin doesn't exist without guilt, its emotional counterpart.

When you accept Christ as your personal Savior and Lord, you are freed from the state of sin and guilt. From time to time you may sin, and when that happens, the Holy Spirit brings a conviction that a wrong has been committed before the Father. Guilt is the warning bell that sin has taken place. Guilt should be the signal for you to go to the Father and say, "I have sinned. Please cleanse me of this, and help me never to do this again."

If you are slow in responding to guilt, allowing it to build up, you may fall into the trap of thinking, "I'm a Christian who should have known better. I don't see how God can forgive me." Or, "I keep committing this same sin. God is not going to forgive me this time." Or, "God knows my weakness, and since He hasn't changed this part of me, He must know that I'm going to continue to sin in this way." Or even, "I've waited too long to ask for God's forgiveness."

All of these lines of reasoning are in error. God always stands ready to forgive when you come to Him with a contrite heart. When you sin, you must go *immediately* to your loving heavenly Father and ask Him to cleanse you, renew you, and help you not to sin further.

1. "If we say that we have no sin, we deceive ourselves, and the truth is not in us. If we confess our sins, He is faithful and just to forgive us our sins and to cleanse us from all unrighteousness"

(1 John 1:8–9). Why is it important to confess our sins? What happens when a believer in Christ does not confess his or her sins?

....

....

....

....

....

....

....

2. "Since we are surrounded by so great a cloud of witnesses, let us lay aside every weight, and the sin which so easily ensnares us, and let us run with endurance the race that is set before us" (Hebrews 12:1). What sort of "weights" hinder a Christian's walk with God? What is required to "lay aside" those weights?

....

....

....

....

....

....

....

....

THREE TYPES OF GUILT

The direction of guilt tends to fall into these categories: (1) *guilt toward God*—you feel guilty because you have never sought God's forgiveness or, as a Christian, you have sinned against God; (2) *guilt toward others*—you feel guilty because you have sinned against another person; or (3) *guilt toward yourself*—what is known as "false guilt."

False guilt occurs when you manufacture a feeling of guilt for something you erroneously assume you have done, or for something in which you feel you have had a part. For example, a young woman may feel guilty for having been the victim of incest, rape, or sexual abuse. Even though she is an innocent victim, she falsely assumes that she bears responsibility for the sin. Or she may feel she did something to bring about the sin or contribute to it. She feels guilt even though, before God, she is innocent.

Many people carry false guilt with them from their childhood. They feel guilty for their parents' divorce, the illness of a grandparent, an injury to a sibling—even though they were not responsible for what transpired. False guilt is as real as guilt for sins. It feels the same, and it bears the same consequences. The difference is that false guilt ends up being directed at *yourself*, and false guilt is *not* directly linked to sin. False guilt is guilt without sin.

3. "Do not be conformed to this world, but be transformed by the renewing of your mind, that you may prove what is that good and acceptable and perfect will of God" (Romans 12:2). What is involved in the "renewing of your mind"? How is it accomplished?

....

....

....

....

....

....

4. How can a renewed mind help you "prove" false guilt versus legitimate guilt? How can this set you free from false guilt?

....

....

....

....

....

....

RESULTS OF GUILT

A load of guilt will affect people's behavior in many ways. *First, it manifests in a refusal to succeed.* Those suffering with guilt tend to undermine their own success, feeling unworthy of it in the light of what they have done. *Second, it results in a low energy level.* Guilt saps energy. The mind continues to be weighed down with memories of the sin. The person doesn't exhibit the ambition or fortitude to move forward or to attempt new challenges.

Third, it brings a loss of joy and peace. Those who feel guilty do not know deep, inner contentment. They feel frustrated. There is a restlessness in the spirit and emotions until forgiveness is received. *Fourth, it leads to self-punishment.* Guilty people, feeling of little use and unworthy of blessing, often try to punish themselves. In some cases, they do this to try to avert what they believe would be God's punishment.

Fifth, it brings feelings of insecurity. The guilty feel insecure in their relationship with God. The one who has sinned against another person feels insecure in his relationship with that person. The person who suffers from false guilt tends to feel insecure in a general sense.

Sixth, it can lead to physical problems. Guilt carried for long periods of time grinds away at the heart and mind. Eventually, that grinding stone affects the physical body. Feeling unworthy, the guilty person readily engages in physically negative behaviors—addictions, excesses, and a general failure to be concerned about health.

Seventh, it motivates the guilty to increased "works, works, works." Those who feel guilt sometimes displays a burst of activity they hope will be perceived as good—a heavy dose of voluntary goodness to balance the sin committed. This is false recompense because it doesn't involve genuine forgiveness from God or others.

Finally, it creates a lack of interest in prayer or involvement in ministry activities. The guilty parties do not think God will hear them, bless them, or respond to them. Therefore, they cease their attempts to communicate with Him. The ultimate consequence of guilt, of course, is that people are in danger of losing their souls. The more they shut themselves off from God the more they isolate themselves from forgiveness and wholeness. The resulting state is misery and isolation.

If you are carrying a load of guilt today, you need to recognize you may wear a mask that is effective in hiding your guilt from others, but you cannot stop its deadly consequences from occurring on the inside. You need to respond by facing your sin and owning up to it, and then receive God's forgiveness. If you are carrying a load of false guilt, you need to come to grips with the truth of your situation.

5. "When I kept silent, my bones grew old through my groaning all the day long. For day and night Your hand was heavy upon me; my vitality was turned into the drought of summer" (Psalm 32:3–4). What was the effect in David's life when he failed to confess his sin? When have you experienced something similar?

6. "I acknowledged my sin to You, and my iniquity I have not hidden. I said, 'I will confess my transgressions to the LORD,' and You forgave the iniquity of my sin" (Psalm 32:5). What was the result when David chose to confess his sin to the Lord?

STEPS FOR BEING FREE OF GUILT

We have touched on several of the key steps required to be free of guilt, all of which fall under the banner of forgiveness. These steps are as follows. *First, face up to the sin that resulted in your guilt.* Admit your sin to God. If you have sinned against another person, confess to that person that you have sinned against him or her. In facing up to your sin, make certain that it is a sin before God. The sin that you think you have committed may have been a mistake or somebody else's sin.

Second, acknowledge you made a mistake. Unless you have done something willful to rebel against God's Word or to breach your relationship, you have made a mistake. You can apologize for mistakes and ask God to help you not repeat the same errors. You can commit yourself to a new start. Our society is quick to dismiss as "normal" some behaviors that are against God's Word. The Bible presents a clear picture of what is considered sin and what is not. If you have any doubt about whether you have sinned, consult the Scriptures.

Third, don't take blame for somebody else's sin. Own up to any role you may have played in a sinful event, but don't assume blame for something not your fault. You may want to consult someone who can provide godly counsel about whether you have fault in a situation. Make sure the advice is in line with the Bible. When you confess to God or a person that you have sinned, don't try to justify what you did. Simply state your error and ask for forgiveness

Fourth, make amends. If you have wronged another person, don't merely try to substitute a request for forgiveness by doing kind deeds for the person. (This same principle holds for your relationship with God.) In seeking to make amends for a wrong committed against others, you may be wise to ask them what they would consider to be a fair compensation for the hurt or injury, or you may want to offer compensation of some type. The best compensation may be a genuine change in your life. Ask God to give you wisdom in identifying appropriate amends. Also ask Him to give you the courage and the fortitude to follow through on your commitment to the offended parties and to yourself.

Fifth, accept forgiveness. If you have sinned against God and have repented, you can be assured that He forgives you. His Word promises that He will, and God is always faithful to His Word. If you have sinned against others and they forgive you, accept their words of forgiveness at face value. Don't try to second-guess their sincerity or motives. If the other party *refuses* to forgive you, remember that they bear the responsibility for failing to forgive. You have done what the Lord requires of you, and you stand clear before Him. In the case of false guilt, ask God to erase all feelings of the guilt and heal you of any damage it has caused. Ask Him to help you to forgive yourself fully and to move forward in your life.

Sixth, weave this experience into an area of service to others. Use your experience as a foundation stone in helping others. This way, you turn a negative into a positive. When you help others who have sinned in a similar way, or who are in danger of sinning as you have, you become a blessing to them. In no way is this a compensation for your past. Rather, it is an expression that you truly have received God's forgiveness and you are going forward in your life to love and help others. Your witness must not exalt or attempt to exonerate your own past error but only point others to the saving grace and love of God.

Seventh, praise God for His generous forgiveness. Your heavenly Father is worthy of your constant praise, and certainly so when it comes to your redemption—your salvation, ongoing transformation into the likeness of Christ, spiritual growth, and development. Praise is part of *receiving* forgiveness. It is a sign to yourself, to God, and to others that you truly have accepted God's forgiveness and have forgiven yourself. Praise God, too, when others forgive you. It is an expression of God's forgiveness every time another person forgives you.

7. "Confess your trespasses to one another, and pray for one another, that you may be healed" (James 5:16). What role does prayer play in asking someone for forgiveness? What role does it play in forgiving someone who has wronged you?

....

....

....

....

....

....

8. "Brethren, if anyone among you wanders from the truth, and someone turns him back, let him know that he who turns a sinner from the error of his way will save a soul from death and cover a multitude of sins" (James 5:19–20). What is involved in turning a person away from sin? How is this done in a loving way?

....

....

....

....

....

....

HOW MUCH WILL GOD FORGIVE?

Can we always count on God's forgiveness? Yes, always. God will forgive us of our sins committed against Him. He will forgive us of our trespasses against others. He will strengthen us as we confess our sin to others and ask for their forgiveness. He will heal us of false guilt and help us to put the sins of others completely into the forgiven past.

In the Gospels, we read how one day Peter asked Jesus, "Lord, how often shall my brother sin against me, and I forgive him? Up to seven times?" Jesus replied, "I do not say to you, up to seven times, but up to seventy times seven" (Matthew 18:21-22). This number—*seventy times seven*—refers to an unlimited perfection of forgiveness. We are to forgive others without end. Jesus would not ask Peter to do something that God would not do. Our Father holds out unlimited forgiveness to us. We need to come to Him and receive it.

This does not give us license to sin. People make a serious error when they think they can sin because they can always come to God for forgiveness. Those who think salvation gives them permission to sin may not have experienced a true spiritual conversion. In addition, people who repeatedly sin and then seek forgiveness develop a hardened heart—a callous attitude toward their behavior and a cavalier attitude toward God's mercy. People who sin must face the consequences for their sins.

The Lord chastises those who sin until they seek forgiveness. The consequences of sin are related to the perfection of God's law. The soul may be cleansed and redeemed, but people reap what they sow in their bodies, relationships, material possessions, and other areas of the natural life. As Paul writes, "Do not be deceived: 'Evil company corrupts good habits.' Awake to righteousness, and do not sin" (1 Corinthians 15:33-34).

9. "Be kind to one another, tenderhearted, forgiving one another, even as God in Christ forgave you" (Ephesians 4:32). What promise do we receive about God's forgiveness? How should that shape our attitude toward those who have wronged us?

....

....

....

....

....

....

....

....

10. "Jesus said to him, 'I do not say to you, [forgive] up to seven times, but up to seventy times seven' (Matthew 18:22). Has anyone ever sinned against you 490 times? Have you sinned against God 490 times? What principle is Jesus is teaching in this verse?

....

....

....

....

....

....

....

....

....

....

....

....

....

....

....

....

....

TODAY AND TOMORROW

Today: God not only forgives my sin but can also
make something good out of it!

Tomorrow: I will praise God this week for his endless
grace toward me.

CLOSING PRAYER

Lord Jesus, we recognize that we will never fully understand the depth of Your forgiveness—how we can sin time and again and You are always willing to forgive us. We know that You never preached anything You didn't practice, and when You told Peter to forgive others an infinite number of times, You were telling us that God will continually forgive us when we stumble into sin. We pray today that guilt will never get in the way of us confessing our failures to You—for Your Word says that You are always merciful and ready to extend grace to those who seek it.

NOTES AND PRAYER REQUESTS

Use this space to write any key points, questions, or prayer requests from this week's study.

THE ACID OF ANGER

Learning: When is anger justified?

Growing: What should I do when someone makes me angry?

Few people in Scripture exhibited as much anger as King Saul in his jealousy over the blessings of God in David's life. Saul's anger was triggered when David returned from battle and the women greeted him with this song: "Saul has slain his thousands, and David his ten thousands." The Bible states, "Saul was very angry, and the saying displeased him" (1 Samuel 18:7–8).

In his anger and jealousy, Saul twice threw his spear at David, trying to pin him to the wall (see 18:10–11; 19:9–10). He pursued David for more than a decade, forcing him to live in exile (see 24:1–22; 26:1–25). He chased after David without mercy and ordered the murder of those who helped him. Saul even turned on his own son, Jonathan, with murderous intent (see 20:30). Saul's anger had no end.

It is easy to see anger at work in a person such as Saul. We tolerate a great deal of anger in our personal lives, families, and neighborhoods. Some even see anger as a sign of strength or power. This tolerance for anger is contrary to God's Word, and it is damaging to our emotional health and well-being. It is also damaging to our spiritual growth and witness. The Bible admonishes us, "Do not let the sun go down on your wrath, nor give place to the devil" (Ephesians 4:26–27). Wrath is linked closely with the work of the evil one in our lives.

1. "So the women sang as they danced, and said: 'Saul has slain his thousands, and David his ten thousands.' Then Saul was very angry, and the saying displeased him" (1 Samuel 18:7–8). Why do you think Saul was provoked to anger when he heard this song?

   ....

   ....

   ....

   ....

2. "'Be angry, and do not sin': do not let the sun go down on your wrath, nor give place to the devil" (Ephesians 4:26–27). Why do you think Paul connects *anger* with *sin* in this passage? What does it mean to "not let the sun go down on your wrath"?

   ....

   ....

   ....

   ....

THE CAUSES OF ANGER

Anger is a sudden feeling of displeasure and antagonism in response to an irritating factor. The irritation may be created by another individual or a situation. The angry person may have felt the irritation for some time, but the outburst erupts suddenly. It is not a planned response. The angry person is momentarily out of control—and no longer operating according to reason or God's principles of love.

People become angry because they aren't allowed to have their own way, they are in pain (physical or emotional), or they are jealous of others. In fact, people can become so jealous of other people's possessions, position in life, privileges, and personal traits (such as appearance and personality) that they feel another person's good fortune somehow causes their own bad fortune.

Intense jealousy and anger manifest themselves in similar ways—with explosive, erratic, sometimes violent, and always irrational overtones. Intensely jealous people are also angry people. Ultimately, angry people seek to get rid of the attacker. They sometimes resort to physical violence. In other cases, they put distance between themselves and the persons causing the irritation.

3. "So David played music with his hand, as at other times; but there was a spear in Saul's hand. And Saul cast the spear, for he said, 'I will pin David to the wall!'" (1 Samuel 18:10–11). How did Saul's jealousy over David's success manifest in this passage? Why do you think Saul reacted in this way?

4. What are some "irritating factors" or situations that tend to make you angry? How do you respond when you are faced with these factors or situations?

How Anger Is Expressed

Anger is usually expressed in one of two ways. *First, anger is expressed as a physical or verbal outburst.* A person may throw a punch, pound a fist against the wall, slam a door, swear, shout, or respond with other physical actions. Anger may even manifest itself as gossip. Every form of abuse that I can name—sexual, physical, emotional, verbal—has anger at its root.

Second, anger is expressed as a brooding silence. The person internalizes the anger and allows it to seep into the subconscious. Sometimes this anger displays itself as boredom or an aloofness from other people. The person who broods in silent anger may erupt in anger at a later date. The anger may even erupt within the body in the form of disease. Unless one deals positively and in a godly way with anger, it will manifest itself in some way.

Nothing good comes from anger—which is why it is contrary to God's plan for emotional wholeness. Outbursts of anger injure other people. Internalized anger injures the angry person. Both expressions of anger are closely linked to hatred. Thus, anger is diametrically opposed to love. When we are angry, we cannot respond with sensitivity to the needs of others. We lose our ability to feel compassion. We cause estrangement. We create strife and enmity in relationships. We cease to give generously. And we require unrealistically high standards of behavior from others to compensate for the way that we have been injured or attacked.

These qualities are certainly not Christlike. You may ask, "But what about the little moments of anger that we all feel from time to time?" People who ask this are usually referring to brief outbursts of anger or day-long pouts. All these expressions of anger are equally wrong before God. So ask God to forgive you for *all* expressions of anger against other people and to cleanse you of an angry spirit. Then ask the Holy Spirit to fill you with His love, joy, and peace so that you can manifest these and all the other emotional fruit of the Spirit.

5. "Let every man be swift to hear, slow to speak, slow to wrath; for the wrath of man does not produce the righteousness of God" (James 1:19–20). Why does James link speech with wrath? How do our words increase or decrease our anger?

....

....

....

....

....

6. Which way do you generally deal with anger: *outward eruptions* or *brooding silence*? What are the affects you have witnessed in responding in this manner?

....

....

....

....

RIGHTEOUS INDIGNATION

Some people attempt to justify their anger under the banner of righteous indignation. They point to the behavior of Jesus when He drove the money changers from the temple. They conclude, "I can be angry because Jesus was angry." Let's look at that incident more closely:

> Then Jesus went into the temple of God and drove out all those who bought and sold in the temple, and overturned the tables of the money changers and the seats of those who sold doves. And He said to them, "It is written, 'My house shall be called a house of prayer,' but you have made it a 'den of thieves.'" Then the blind and the lame came to Him in the temple, and He healed them (Matthew 21:12–14; see also Mark 11:15–17 and Luke 19:45–46).

Artists through the centuries have typically depicted Jesus with whip whirling and eyes blazing as He cleanses the temple. He is given every appearance of being an angry and violent man. But this isn't what the Scriptures say. The effects of Jesus' actions did overturn the tables of the money changers, but His actions were calculated. Nobody was out of control. Jesus engaged in a healing service immediately after those who were buying and selling in the temple had been removed. Jesus' righteous indignation was completely without sin and without any diminishing of His spiritual anointing.

Throughout the scene in the temple, we see that Jesus' behavior was *without violence*, *without resentment*, and *without bitterness*. Jesus' action was vented not against individuals but against their actions and against the system that allowed buying and selling in God's house of prayer. Jesus was angry in a righteous way. He did not sin in what He did or the way that He did it. His righteous indignation was a healthy response to evil. It was an agitation in the spirit against something that was wrong in God's eyes, without any partiality toward the perpetrators.

Righteous indignation is thus expressed in a measured and calculated way. It does not bring physical or emotional harm to another human being. It is thought through in a rational way, and it has been pre-approved by God through prayer. Throughout the Scriptures, we are admonished to speak God's truth boldly in such a manner and to do so in love. I believe that is what Jesus was doing in the temple. His words bore great conviction because they were a statement of truth. When we speak the truth boldly, we can also expect results.

Of course, when you take an action or speak the truth with righteous indignation, you must be prepared to reap the consequences. Righteous indignation requires you to put your life on the line for what you believe. The angry person doesn't do this. To the contrary, an angry person acts in hopes of destroying an enemy. The angry person isn't at all interested in suffering or dying for the person who has done wrong in his or her eyes.

7. "God is a just judge, and God is angry with the wicked every day. If he does not turn back, He will sharpen His sword; He bends His bow and makes it ready" (Psalm 7:11–12). How does the psalmist describe God's righteous anger in this passage?

....

....

....

....

8. "And whenever you stand praying, if you have anything against anyone, forgive him, that your Father in heaven may also forgive you your trespasses. But if you do not forgive, neither will your Father in heaven forgive your trespasses" (Mark 11:25–26). What is the greatest danger of harboring anger toward someone?

....

....

....

....

NEUTRALIZING THE ACID OF ANGER

Unchecked anger acts as acid on the soul—eating away at your spirit and eventually destroying all feelings of love toward others. You must neutralize anger as soon as you are aware of it. If you don't, you may very well repress it (which is dangerous to you physically and emotionally), suppress it (which is like burying anger alive), or express it, (in a way that is hurtful to others).

How do you neutralize anger? *First, confess it.* Admit to God that you are angry. Ask for His forgiveness, help, and healing. If you have expressed your anger to another person, go to that individual and confess that you have acted in a way contrary to God's plan. Ask the person's forgiveness. Once you have confessed your sin to the person, just walk away. Thank God for His forgiveness!

Second, choose to trust God fully. Many people who are angry with others are actually angry with God for something they think He has done to them or failed to do for them. The reality is that if you are angry with God, you cannot trust God. The cycle is deadly, and the consequences may be eternal. Deep anger at God can keep a person out of heaven. Don't let that happen!

Confess your anger to God, and ask Him to forgive you for it. Make a commitment in your heart to trust God with your entire life, and in following through on that commitment, ask the Holy Spirit daily to lead you, guide you, and protect you from all evil. Also, go to God's Word and read verses that promise God's sure and ready help to His children.

9. "Beloved, do not avenge yourselves, but rather give place to wrath; for it is written, 'Vengeance is Mine, I will repay,' says the Lord" (Romans 12:19). When have you taken revenge on another person? What was the long-term result?

....

....

....

....

....

10. "Therefore 'if your enemy is hungry, feed him; if he is thirsty, give him a drink' for in so doing you will heap coals of fire on his head'" (Romans 12:20). What does it mean to "heap coals of fire" on another person's head?

....

....

....

....

....

TODAY AND TOMORROW

Today: My unjustified anger can prevent me from reflecting God's righteousness to others.

Tomorrow: I will ask the Lord this week to dig out the roots of anger in my life.

CLOSING PRAYER

Father, thank You for loving us. Thank You for not getting angry with Your children. You watch us almost destroy our lives and ruin the wonderful things You've sent because we can't control this emotion called anger. We let it become bitterness and resentfulness and aggression toward others. Forgive us for allowing our anger to result in sin, and help us to refuse to carry this negative emotion inside us like a timebomb . . . just ready to go off. Thank You for being gentle with us and for showing us the way to live at peace.

Notes and Prayer Requests

· ·

Use this space to write any key points, questions, or prayer requests from this week's study.

THE REPROACH OF REJECTION

IN THIS LESSON

Learning: Why do people reject me?

Growing: How can I avoid rejection and learn from it at the same time?

Rejection is a form of loneliness. It is estrangement and isolation from others who have willfully removed themselves from your presence. Rejection hurts just as loneliness hurts, but the pain is different. With loneliness, you feel sorrow and sadness that you are alone and separated from fellowship. With rejection, the pain is like that of a rusty, dull knife stabbed into the heart. The feeling is one of intense pain accompanied by worthlessness. The rejected person readily concludes, "Nobody loves me, nobody understands me, and nobody wants to be around me."

Those who allow rejection to go unchecked transfer their feelings of rejection to all people. They make a basic assumption that *everybody* is going to reject them. With this attitude, they make themselves less approachable, less likable (since new acquaintances are made to feel badly for something they haven't done), and more vulnerable to further rejection. The cycle is negative ... as are all the negative emotions discussed in this study guide.

Rejection can result in *over-sensitivity*—your feelings are hurt far too easily. It can lead to *bitterness* at the person who rejected you, *resentment* (especially toward those who are *not* rejected by others), and *suspicion* of others. You may start expecting only bad things in life to happen and become suspicious of any person who acts kindly toward you. You may feel that you are being set up for a fall by every person you encounter.

Rejection can also lead to *isolation*—you may choose to separate yourself from others so you will not be hurt by them. This can make you appear aloof, emotionally distant, or egotistical. It can result in *self-criticism*—you may put yourself down and compare yourself unfavorably to others. It can also lead to *guilt*—you assume that you are worthy to be rejected. You may respond by doing everything in your power to prove to yourself and others, "I am someone!" Sometimes this involves changes in appearance, acquisition of status-related possessions, a constant striving for achievement, or perfectionist behavior.

No two people react to rejection in exactly the same way. The behaviors that manifest rejection, however, are potentially damaging in that they fail to deal with the underlying issue, and they create situations that require further healing for the person to become emotionally whole. Dealing with rejection is difficult enough without compounding rejection with resentment, bitterness, guilt, egocentric behavior, or a critical spirit.

1. When have you felt rejected? How did you respond?

....

....

....

....

....

2. Which of the above responses have you used during times of rejection in the past? What resulted from those responses?

....

....

....

....

....

THE SOURCES OF REJECTION

Rejection arises from one of three sources. *The first is parents' failure to provide expressions of love.* If children do not receive needed expressions of love, they grow up feeling that something is missing or that they were unworthy of receiving all that they needed. Children's need for love is just as strong as the basic needs for food and shelter.

Children have different capacities for love and require love expressed in varying forms. One child may perceive love in terms of hugs and kisses. Another child may feel smothered by hugs and kisses and perceive that a parent is loving if he or she provides a sense of freedom of movement. For this reason, parents must be sensitive to their children's unique personality and need for love.

The second source is criticism from others. Criticism precedes acts of alienation. A person tends to move away from another person because being around the other person is undesirable, unhealthful, or dangerous. These are critical evaluations. The rejected person feels the isolation when it occurs and also the underlying criticism.

Just as with the root causes of anger, those feeling rejected may suffer from errors of perception. They may perceive their parents failed to love them, even though the parents did everything they could to express their love. They may perceive another person has rejected them, when the person just wanted some "alone time." Perception governs feelings of rejection. The rejected person feels great pain whether it is real or imagined.

Furthermore, the sting of criticism associated with rejection may actually be unwarranted criticism. The person who is doing the rejecting may be thinking in error or under emotional illness. Sometimes, people level criticism at others out of insecurity, jealousy, guilt, or weakness. They project their own failures onto the nearest target and fire off critical comments to make themselves feel better.

Once such individuals have registered such intense criticism, rejection naturally follows. It is very difficult for a person who has seriously criticized another to turn around and openly embrace that person. Meanwhile, the rejected person has little recourse. He can do nothing to turn the tide of criticism or to keep the rejection from happening. A feeling of victimization can take over if the rejected person doesn't seek God's healing.

A third source of rejection is self-rejection. This is perhaps the most damaging to one's emotional well-being. When self-rejection is at the root of the problem, people assume that they are worthy of being rejected. So, rather than waiting for others to reject them, they isolate themselves from others, become self-critical, seek self-validation, and strive for perfection.

Self-rejection nearly always arises from feelings of guilt associated with sin. Those who commit sin against God or others usually try to put distance between themselves and God or the offended parties. If you are engaging in this unhealthful emotional response of self-rejection, reread the lesson on guilt. There is something related to sin and forgiveness with which you haven't dealt . . . or you may be in self-rejection because of false guilt.

You may find it difficult to recognize that your feelings of rejection are the product of your own behavior. If so, you may need to discuss this with a godly counselor who bases his or her advice on God's Word.

3. "All that the Father gives Me will come to Me, and the one who comes to Me I will by no means cast out" (John 6:37). Have you come to Christ to find acceptance before God? If so, how does God's acceptance of you override what other people think?

....

....

....

....

....

4. "For no one ever hated his own flesh, but nourishes and cherishes it, just as the Lord does the church. For we are members of His body, of His flesh and of His bones" (Ephesians 5:29–30). If no one truly hates his own flesh, what does this suggest about self-rejection? What should your attitude be toward yourself?

....

....

....

....

....

INITIAL STEPS TO MOVE OUT OF REJECTION

There are at least six things you must do to recover from feelings of rejection. *First, recognize the source of the rejection.* Identify specifically who has rejected you. If you have vague feelings of rejection, talk to a godly person about them. Your rejection is related to something that someone (or a group of people) has done or said. As you identify the source, remember that God never rejects you! He always is available to you with open arms and a heart of love.

Second, separate the person's rejection of you and the rejection of your deeds. This is especially important if you have been rejected because of your witness of Christ or for something good you did. If love was your motivation, you are in right standing with God. Some people cannot accept good from others. Their unworthiness causes them to reject those who bless them. In like manner, those who haven't accepted Jesus find it difficult to accept those who are Christians. They aren't rejecting you solely; they are also rejecting God.

In cases where you know you have done something bad and rejection is a response to your behavior, own up to what you have done. Confess your wrong to God and to others. Make amends when possible. Accept God's forgiveness and make a commitment to better behavior. But never draw the conclusion that you are a bad person who cannot be redeemed or forgiven. To God, you are always of infinite value. God's love for you has no bounds. You may have acted in a sinful way, but you are not beyond God's ability to forgive you. So admit what you are feeling and receive God's forgiveness.

Third, reject the rejection. In the final analysis, only God's opinion of you counts. He never rejects you. Once you are forgiven by God, you stand in a cleansed state before Him. No amount of dirt that others throw at you in the form of criticism should be allowed to stick. In the face of criticism and rejection, you need to proclaim with boldness to your spirit, "I am accepted, loved, and forgiven by God, and His response is all that matters!"

The apostle Paul wrote, "[I] do not cease to give thanks for you, making mention of you in my prayers: that the God of our Lord Jesus Christ, the Father of glory, may give to you the spirit of wisdom and revelation in the knowledge of Him, the eyes of your understanding being enlightened; that you may know what is the hope of His calling, what are the riches of the glory of His inheritance in the saints, and what is the exceeding greatness of His power toward us who believe" (Ephesians 1:16–19). Paul wanted the believers in Ephesus to know these things about themselves . . . and you are to know these things about yourself as well.

First, you have the hope of God's calling. God wants you not to be isolated or filled with feelings of rejection. Rather, He desires that you might have hope for the future—that you will enjoy deep and abiding friendships with other Christians whom the Lord brings into your life so that together you might fulfill God's plan on earth. God designed His church to function as a body, and that means God has a role for you to fulfill. His purpose for you is not *rejection* but *fulfillment* in loving relationships with other Christians.

Second, you have the riches of the glory of God's inheritance. There is no eternal blessing that God withholds from any person who proclaims Jesus as Lord. *Finally, you have the exceeding greatness of His power.* Trust God to deal with those who have rejected you falsely—to enlighten them in their error, convict them of their criticism, and move in their hearts so they will treat you with kindness in the future. God is able and willing to do this. Ask Him to work on your behalf so that all things in your life will come to a good and fruitful end.

5. What is a situation in your life in which you need to *identify the source of rejection, separate others' rejection of you from your deeds,* and *reject the rejection?* Explain.

....

....

....

....

....

....

....

....

....

6. "Do you not know that your body is the temple of the Holy Spirit who is in you, whom you have from God, and you are not your own?" (1 Corinthians 6:19). What does this say about the way God sees you? Why is His opinion the only one that matters?

....

....

....

....

....

....

....

....

....

7. "I bow my knees to the Father . . . that you, being rooted and grounded in love, may be able to comprehend with all the saints what is the width and length and depth and height to know the love of Christ which passes knowledge; that you may be filled with all the fullness of God" (Ephesians 3:14, 17–19). What is required if you are to "know the love of Christ" in your life? What does it mean to be "filled with all the fullness of God"?

....

....

....

....

....

....

....

....

....

FURTHER STEPS TO MOVE OUT OF REJECTION

The fourth step to take to move out of rejection is to forgive the person who has rejected you. You need to identify the person who caused your feelings of rejection (step 1) so you can forgive that person. You must also forgive any person who has erroneously taught you that God may have rejected you. Forgiveness does not mean the person's behavior was right or that it didn't hurt. Forgiveness just means letting the offending party go.

In exercising forgiveness, you are freeing the offending persons from your heart and entrusting them to God. In freeing them, you become free of them and of their hurtful influence on your life. Those individuals who harmed you are never free, however, from God's watchful eye and from what God will require of them.

The fifth step is put your full focus on God. Concentrate on who God is in your life. He is your Creator, Savior, daily Comforter, and Counselor. He knows everything about you and loves you unconditionally. He can move heaven and earth on your behalf. He is always present and available to you. And He will never reject you or disown you. Even if the entire world seems to reject you, God does not.

So choose to invest in the one relationship in your life that will never be marred by rejection. Spend time with God. Pour out your devotion toward Him. He will bring others into your life who can receive your talents and gifts, love you deeply, and delight in your personality. Immerse yourself in God's Word so that you can understand more fully the almighty God and heavenly Father who is the eternal lover of your soul. Stay in close fellowship with Him.

Finally, give generously to others. The person who gives generously to others is rarely rejected. Turn outward from your rejection to embrace life and to reach out to other people. God does not want you to feel the anguish and reproach of rejection but to experience His love and enjoy the friendship of others who love Christ. For you to be healed of the effects of rejection in your life, you must choose to allow God's love to enter your heart. So open up your life today to Him. Invite Him to do His deep, inner healing work in you.

8. What is a situation in your life in which you need to *forgive the person who has rejected you, put your full focus on God,* and *give generously to others*? Explain.

_____

_____

_____

_____

9. "If we say that we have fellowship with Him, and walk in darkness, we lie and do not practice the truth. But if we walk in the light as He is in the light, we have fellowship with one another, and the blood of Jesus Christ His Son cleanses us from all sin" (1 John 1:6–7). What does it mean to "walk in darkness" and "walk in the light"?

_____

_____

_____

_____

10. How can "walking in the light" of God's Word bring emotional wholeness to you this week?

_____

_____

_____

_____

_____

TODAY AND TOMORROW

Today: God's opinion of me is all that matters,
and He will never reject His children.

Tomorrow: I will reach out to others this week,
giving generously and freely.

CLOSING PRAYER

Jesus, thank You for saying that You will not cast out anyone who comes to You. Thank You that we can know You always accept us and that You are molding and shaping us into the people that You want us to be. I ask You today to help us understand that we are never truly rejected because You are always with us. And help us to reach out to those in our world who are hurting—those who need to know we love them and support them. Let us be Your example in this world of what it means to truly embrace one another in love.

NOTES AND PRAYER REQUESTS

Use this space to write any key points, questions, or prayer requests from this week's study.

THE LONGING
OF LONELINESS

IN THIS LESSON

Learning: What role does loneliness play in my life and
in the lives of those around me?

Growing: What steps can I take to move away from loneliness
and toward the companionship of God and others?

Did you know there are more than fifty definitions for the word *good*
in our modern dictionary? Fifty! There may not be another word
in the English language that we use so freely and so widely to describe
an incredible range of experiences.

I will give you a few examples. You might use the word *good* to
describe a person who is morally upright and virtuous. "She is a good
person." Or, you could use *good* to describe someone who is effective

in terms of quality. "He is a good employee." We also use *good* when referring to someone or something that we believe well-behaved. "That is a good dog."

It goes on. We can use *good* to talk about food or other items that are edible or unspoiled. "We lost power in our refrigerator, but the meat is still good." We can use *good* to describe the quality of a relationship that is intact. "Am I in the doghouse with my wife? No, we're good." And we can even use *good* as a noun to describe commodities. "We sell a wide variety of goods and services."

Obviously, the Bible has a lot to say about goodness, since we know that God Himself is the standard for what is good— He alone is good (see Mark 10:18). But as we continue in this study of becoming emotionally whole, I want to focus for a moment on something that God definitively labeled as "not good." We find that moment in Genesis 2.

When you read the story of creation in those opening chapters of the Bible, there is a consistent declaration that stands out immediately. This declaration is that everything God made was "good." After God declared, "Let there be light," the Bible says, "God saw the light, that it was good" (1:3–4). When God gathered the waters around the earth so that dry ground appeared, He again "saw that it was good" (verse 10). When God created the beasts of the earth according to their kinds, He "saw that it was good" (verse 25). And when God looked over everything He had made at the end of the sixth day—including humanity—the Scripture says, "indeed it was very good" (verse 31).

Right away, God was pleased with His creation. When He looked down at the Garden of Eden and observed everything He had designed and brought to life across the entire universe, He was pleased with what He saw. It was "good." This is a major theme of Genesis 1. But when we come to Genesis 2, we read, "The LORD God said, 'It is not good that man should be alone'" (verse 18). *God knows that loneliness is not good.* We need to understand that as well.

1. What's the first thing that comes to mind when you think of the word *loneliness*? Why?

....

....

....

....

2. During what seasons of your life have you experienced loneliness in a significant way?

....

....

....

....

LONELINESS IS AN ATTITUDE

Before we go any further, we need to define *loneliness*. What does it mean to be lonely? The dictionary defines loneliness this way: "Destitute of sympathetic or friendly companionship, support, etc." I think that sounds overly clinical. To me, and to most people, loneliness is best described as simply having less connection and companionship with others than you need.

Loneliness means having fewer meaningful relationships and less significant time with people than you need in order to feel loved, cared for, and valued. In other words, it is more than just being alone. It is more than simply not being around people for a certain amount of time. You can be married and still feel lonely. You can have a lot of acquaintances and be around a lot of people and still feel lonely. Loneliness is an attitude . . . not a matter of geography.

In the Garden of Eden, it seemed as if Adam had everything he needed. He was in paradise! But it quickly became apparent that one thing was missing—and that was somebody else. He needed companionship. Actually, Adam needed more than companionship, because he already had a deep and intimate relationship with God. Yet the Lord still declared that there was something "not good" about the current state of affairs. Adam needed human companionship. He needed Eve to share in his experiences.

As I was thinking about this topic and researching it, I spoke with several people who have experienced loneliness in a significant way. I asked them, "How did you feel at your loneliest moment?" I received many different answers. One person said, "I feel like just crying out for somebody to listen to me." Someone else said, "At my loneliest moment, I feel like I am sitting in a dense fog and I'm batting it and trying to wipe it away. But somehow every time I swing my hand, it just clouds in upon me."

Loneliness is an attitude—and it's not about the number of people around you. Just think of all the women who have said, "I live in the same house as my husband, but somehow he still feels far away." And think of all the men who have said, "My wife and I have been married for years, but somehow I still don't know what happens deep inside her heart." You can be sitting in the middle of a crowded room—or live in the same house with another person for years—and still feel lonely. Loneliness is in the mind.

3. Do you agree that loneliness is based on what's happening inside, rather than the amount of people around you? Explain.

4. What do you typically experience when you are lonely? What does it feel like?

....

....

....

....

....

....

....

REPENT OF YOUR SINS

Now that we understand what loneliness is, we need to address what we do about it. If you are experiencing loneliness, what steps can you take to improve your situation and remove yourself from the longing of loneliness? There are three steps that I recommend you take.

The first step is to repent of your sins. If you want to begin to overcome the problem of loneliness, you need to confess your sins and turn to God. This is especially true if you have never trusted Jesus as your Savior. Why is this such an important first step in moving away from loneliness? Because Jesus knows what you are going through. There is no one in all of history who understands loneliness like Jesus Christ understood it.

Maybe you say, "How could that be if He was the perfect son of God? How could Jesus be lonely if He had fellowship eternally with the Father in Heaven?" The reason is because there came a day when He was nailed to an old, rugged cross, and the only people around Him were the Roman soldiers who placed him there, a crowd who mocked and jeered at Him, and—way out in the distance—His mother and John. All of His disciples had fled on the night of His arrest. His friends had abandoned Him. Yet what broke Him the most was when He experienced that even God—his heavenly Father—had departed from Him.

This is the moment when Jesus cried out, "My God, My God, why have You forsaken Me?" (Matthew 27:46). No man who has ever lived has tasted that kind of loneliness. So, Jesus certainly understands what it means to be lonely. As we read in Hebrews, "We do not have a High Priest who cannot sympathize with our weaknesses, but was in all points tempted as we are, yet without sin" (Hebrews 4:15).

As you come to comprehend the full weight of this verse, you come to realize that Jesus experienced every feeling that you will ever have. Jesus has experienced all the emotions you deal with and have to work through and process through each day. And He understands what it means to be lonely, because for a moment He was left all alone without God. Thus, if you are seeking to move away from loneliness, your first step is to repent of your sins and turn toward Jesus. Because He knows. He understands. And He can help.

5. What are ways that loneliness can impact our spiritual lives?

6. What does it mean to you to know that Jesus has experienced every emotion that you will ever face—including loneliness?

RECALL GOD'S PROMISES

The second step in moving away from loneliness is to recall the promises of God. You need to remember what God has promised through His Word and how those promises apply to your life specifically. For the truth is that the promises of God in the Bible always apply to your life.

For example, think about Jesus' words in John 16:32, when He said, "Indeed the hour is coming, yes, has now come, that you will be scattered, each to his own, and will leave Me alone. And yet I am not alone, because the Father is with Me." What was true of Jesus is true for us as well—namely, that God is with us. Always. In every moment. If you are struggling with loneliness in any way, you need to do everything possible to get that message into your heart: God is with you. "For He Himself has said, 'I will never leave you nor forsake you'" (Hebrews 13:5).

Jesus makes a similar promise in John 14:16: "And I will pray the Father, and He will give you another Helper, that He may abide with you forever." Did you know that, as a Christian, it is absolutely impossible for you to be alone? The day you accepted Jesus Christ as your personal savior, you slammed the door on being alone, forever. This is because the Holy Spirit now abides within you. According to this verse, He will remain with you always . . . forever.

The psalmist asked, "Where can I go from Your Spirit? Or where can I flee from Your presence?" (Psalm 139:7). The answer was *nowhere.* There is no place you can go and nothing you can do that will separate you from God. God is with you all the time.

So remember these promises when you are tempted toward loneliness. Remember these truths whenever you feel isolated or separated from others. Yes, you still need human relationships, as was the case with Adam. But when you have an intimate connection with God, it becomes the foundation and the fountain that will sustain you even through times when you aren't as connected with other people as you would like to be.

7. What are some biblical promises that have been important in your spiritual life? Why?

....

....

....

....

....

....

8. How can you remind yourself about God's promises when you are confronted by feelings of loneliness?

....

....

....

....

....

....

REVEAL YOURSELF IN RELATIONSHIPS

The final step in moving away from loneliness is to open your heart to someone. As I just mentioned, your fellowship with God can sustain your need for companionship through long periods when you feel the weight of loneliness. Ultimately, though, you need to build significant relationships with other people. This is because you were created to function within those relationships.

So, it is important for you to find somebody with whom you can connect . . . or find multiple someones in your life. You may feel like they will not understand you, but open your heart anyway. If you can open your heart to somebody, there is something about that action that drives loneliness away, even if the other person does not fully understand you. Reveal yourself to others and put in the work to establish relationships.

Trust me when I say there is somebody out there with whom you can build a relationship. The church can help. In fact, the church should be the first place that someone can go to and find significant relationships. We are a family, after all. The family of God.

Don't let yourself get introspective and pulled inward. Don't allow yourself to say, "I'm a nobody, and nobody wants to know me." That idea is false. In fact, I will tell you how great you are. You're great enough for God to have chosen to inhabit you, to love you, to dwell with you, and abide with you forever. This means you are somebody of worth and of value to God—and that means you are somebody of worth and value, period!

Let me leave you with one last thought. I believe the greatest weapon against loneliness is to reach out and *serve* somebody else. It doesn't make any difference what your circumstances may be. If you can reach out in some way and serve somebody—to just do something for somebody else—it will do more to bring you victory over loneliness than anything else. If you can reach out and meet someone else's needs, you will see your own loneliness vanish. You will find a contentment in your life like you have never known before.

9. "And let us consider one another in order to stir up love and good works, not forsaking the assembling of ourselves together" (Hebrews 10:24–25). How should those in the church interact with one another? How does this combat loneliness?

10. Where do you currently have opportunities to "stir up love and good works" and actively serve other people?

....

....

....

....

....

REACHING OUT TO THE LONELY

As we conclude this lesson, I realize it is possible that you might be thinking, "I don't struggle with loneliness. So what does this subject have to do with me?" The answer is that this topic has a great deal to do with you.

There are people all over this country, in your city, and right in your church who are dying on the inside because they are lonely and empty. Just think of what that means for those people . . . and especially for those who don't yet know Christ. Imagine what a lost person suffers who struggles with loneliness and has no concept of the revelation and the presence and the power and the love of God in their heart.

In our busy world, it's easy to become so insensitive to those who are crying out all around us—crying out for companionship. What they need is for somebody to listen and somebody to care. It often seems that everybody is so involved with their own lives that there is no time to listen to anybody else. This is a shame within the family of God. It is a failure.

Do you know what lonely people need? Just a friend. That's all. And do you know the kind of friend they need? The kind of friend like you and me. They need somebody who is willing to listen and take time for them. As Christians, we will never be able to stand before God without regret if we run through life too busy to listen to somebody who is crying out for help. In fact, we can knock on doors and share our faith until hundreds have responded to the call of salvation in Christ Jesus. But if we've stepped on, walked by, and shoved aside even a dozen lonely people, we will have missed out on a valuable opportunity to show God's love to the world.

Isn't the church the body of Jesus Christ? Aren't we a part of the family of God? No part of the family ought to allow any other part of the family to be lonely. God put us here to give ourselves to one another and to meet the needs of one another. This is everyone's job . . . including yours and mine.

TODAY AND TOMORROW

Today: I don't have to be victimized by loneliness in my life.

Tomorrow: As part of God's family, I will take steps to be a friend to those in need.

CLOSING PRAYER

Heavenly Father, we know that the greatest weapon against loneliness is to reach out and serve someone else. There is something about getting outside of ourselves and focusing on others that helps us to realize we are not alone in what we are facing. Help us today to reach out and seek to meet someone else's needs. Let us experience the joy and contentment that comes from serving others in a selfless manner—just as You modeled to us. Let our churches be a place where people feel needed, accepted, and loved. Let us reflect Your light to the world.

NOTES AND
PRAYER REQUESTS

Use this space to write any key points, questions, or prayer requests from this week's study.

THE DEFEAT OF DISCOURAGEMENT

Learning: What are the roots and consequences of discouragement in my life?

Growing: What steps can I take to defeat seasons of discouragement in my life?

I have a challenge for you as we begin this final lesson. I want you to think back to some of the darker seasons of your life. I am talking about those periods of months or even years when it felt like nothing was going the way you hoped. Nothing was turning out like you planned. Those times when you felt little joy but much sadness.

Can you remember those seasons? I know it's not an enjoyable experience, but can you remember how it felt when you woke up each morning and when you went to bed each night with that darkness still surrounding you? If so, you have a great understanding of why we need to address the topic of discouragement in this final lesson.

So far in this study, we have seen that God is the creator of our emotions and that emotional wholeness is key to a healthy life. We have tackled the ache of anxiety, the grip of fear, and the grindstone of guilt. We have explored the acid of anger, the reproach of rejection, and the longing of loneliness. Now it is time to take a head-on look at *discouragement,* for it often serves as a root to many of our other emotional problems. Dealing with discouragement properly is a critical element in our journey to becoming emotionally whole.

I was talking recently with someone who struggles with intense discouragement, and I asked him what it feels like when he is in the middle of that darkness. He said, "It's like a cloud that hovers over me. I can't identify what it is. I don't know why it's there. I don't know how to get rid of it. I just feel like I'm trapped. Somehow, there's no sense of joy and peace and contentment in my life. I can pray and talk to God, but the cloud doesn't go away."

Can you identify with that imagery? With those thoughts? There is a good chance you answered yes, because discouragement is a universal experience for each of us as human beings. We all get discouraged from time to time, and sometimes that discouragement can deepen and stretch until it feels like that's all we know.

But the message I want to share with you in this lesson is that discouragement can be defeated. It can be resisted and rejected. So don't lose hope!

1. How would you describe your experiences with discouragement?

....

....

....

....

....

....

2. What have been some of the major causes of discouragement in your life?

....

....

....

....

....

....

....

....

THE ROOT OF DISCOURAGEMENT

What causes discouragement in our lives? This is an important question for us to address, because we need to know what causes something if we want to defeat it. So, what brings, welcomes, or allows discouragement into our hearts?

The first point we need to understand is the difference between disappointment and discouragement. Those two are connected in an important way. *Disappointment* is an emotional response to a failed expectation. That is, you might become disappointed when your expectations are not met—when something or someone doesn't measure up to what you had hoped, and what you expected to happen doesn't happen. Thus, disappointment is an emotional response to a failed expectation, desire, or hope.

Discouragement is much deeper—and more serious and sinister. It is a faintness of heart. It is a lack of confidence in ourselves and in the world around us that causes us to feel as if nothing has ever gone right and nothing will ever go right again. It represents an oppressive feeling or a weight that makes us want to give up and quit.

Disappointment always leads to discouragement. All of us experience disappointments. All of us have unmet expectations. All of us have things we wish would happen that don't happen and things we hope will never happen that do happen. We experience this every day! But when that disappointment is unresolved—when it is denied or when we do not deal with it properly—it leads to discouragement.

Here is how it works. Something happens that makes us disappointed—or often it is several disappointments that hit us around the same time. When the disappointment is not dealt with in a positive way, if it's not acknowledged or resolved, it stays with us. Soon, we begin to focus on that disappointment and harbor it deep inside. We hold it close and keep thinking about it. And the longer we think about it, the bigger it grows. And the bigger it grows, the more it leads us into a season of discouragement.

Think about your life. How do you handle disappointments? When someone does something to hurt you, do you address the issue and seek resolution? Or do you sulk? Do you make things bigger than they are? Do you chew on the offense like a dog worrying a bone? The crux of what I'm saying is that disappointments are inevitable. They happen to everyone. But discouragement is a choice. Discouragement is something we allow to develop by choosing to dwell on those disappointments rather than letting them go.

3. What are some disappointments you are dealing with right now or in recent weeks?

....

....

....

....

....

....

....

....

....

4. What is your reaction to the claim that discouragement is a choice? Explain.

....

....

....

....

....

....

....

....

....

....

AN EXAMPLE FROM SCRIPTURE

The story of Nehemiah in the Bible provides an example of how to defeat discouragement. If you are not familiar with Nehemiah, he was a Jewish man in the Old Testament who lived in the Persian city of Shushan and served as cupbearer to the Persian king. He lived during the generation after Jerusalem was sacked and many Jewish people were carried into exile.

At the beginning of the story, Nehemiah learned that not only had Jerusalem been conquered but that its gates and it walls had been torn down. This meant the city was defenseless and had no hope of being rebuilt. Nehemiah was distraught by this news, and he decided to do something about it. After a miraculous conversation with the king of Persia, Nehemiah led a delegation back to Jerusalem with the goal of restoring its walls.

Unfortunately, Nehemiah and the other residents of Jerusalem didn't have an easy go of things once they started rebuilding. They were under constant pressure from their enemies—leaders of the neighboring nations who didn't want to see Jerusalem restored.

Nehemiah said the following about those enemies during a conversation with God:

> Hear, O our God, for we are despised; turn their reproach on their own heads, and give them as plunder to a land of captivity! Do not cover their iniquity, and do not let their sin be blotted out from before You; for they have provoked You to anger before the builders (Nehemiah 4:4–5).

Nehemiah was on a mission from God to restore the walls of Jerusalem. He had the full authority of the king of Babylon behind him. Yet he still had to deal with disappointment! He still had to deal with letdowns and attacks. The same will be true in our lives. Just because we know that God is with us does not mean we will escape going through certain setbacks. The important point is how we *respond*. In Nehemiah's case, he did the following:

> So it was, from that time on, that half of my servants worked at construction, while the other half held the spears, the shields, the bows, and wore armor; and the leaders were behind all the house of Judah. . . .
>
> Every one of the builders had his sword girded at his side as he built. And the one who sounded the trumpet was beside me.
>
> Then I said to the nobles, the rulers, and the rest of the people, "The work is great and extensive, and we are separated far from one another on the wall. Wherever you hear the sound of the trumpet, rally to us there. Our God will fight for us" (Nehemiah 4:16, 18–20).

Nehemiah was hit with many disappointments, but he didn't linger on them. He didn't let them fester. He rallied his people and made sure they didn't allow themselves to slip into discouragement.

5. What do you like best about Nehemiah's leadership in the verses that you have just read?

....
....
....
....
....
....
....
....
....
....

6. Who are some people you can ask to "rally" around you when you are attacked by disappointment or discouragement?

....
....
....
....
....
....
....
....
....

THE CONSEQUENCES OF DISCOURAGEMENT

Nehemiah responded the right way to disappointment and discouragement. But what happens if we respond the *wrong* way? What are the consequences of allowing ourselves to wallow in discouragement?

First, your mind gets divided. A divided mind is that inner gnawing that grabs your attention no matter where you are, who you're with, or what situation you are in.

When you have a divided mind, you cannot focus and do your best. When you are stuck in a pattern of discouragement, you are constantly thinking about what is not right and how you have been wronged. You get stuck thinking about whatever caused your disappointment and all the other ways that you have been disappointed in the past.

Second, you look for somebody to blame. This is basic human nature. Oftentimes, you may start by blaming God: "God, if You're sovereign, You could have kept this from happening. This is Your fault!" Obviously, you will soon find that blaming God in this manner does not accomplish anything, so you will move on to blaming other people in your life. Generally, that is a pretty easy thing to do. It is typically no problem to find someone who let you down and caused the particular crisis you are facing. "I put my faith in them, but they were disloyal. She didn't love me . . . he didn't love me. They walked away. They failed me."

You might then get to the point of blaming yourself. I call this the if-I-had stage. "If I had done this differently, my life would be better. If I had gone there instead of here, I wouldn't be in this mess right now. If I had made a different choice in that situation, I would be in such a better place." The truth is we all make mistakes. But blaming ourselves and festering in a pool of self-hatred doesn't fix anything. It just leads to more discouragement.

Third, you develop anger in your heart. You get angry at God, at others, and at yourself. Unfortunately, anger just makes things worse, because when you develop unresolved anger in your heart, you drive people away. Generally speaking, people are not interested in knowing or fellowshipping with people who live in anger. This will be especially true if you cannot contain that anger and start spewing it on everyone around you.

7. What are some other consequences that you have experienced as the result of discouragement in your life?

....
....
....
....
....
....
....

8. Do you currently see any evidence of a divided mind, blaming others, or anger in your life? Explain.

....
....
....
....
....
....

HOW TO DEFEAT DISCOURAGEMENT

These are just some of the consequences that you will experience if you allow yourself to be discouraged. There are others . . . including the tendency to make bad decisions and drive away those who care about you. The good news is that you don't have to settle for those consequences. You can defeat discouragement and move into a healthy way of life.

When you read Nehemiah's story, it is amazing to find how many times he could have allowed himself to slip into discouragement. Here is just one example. In Nehemiah 5:1–13, the text describes how the wealthier residents of Jerusalem were oppressing the poorer residents by charging them unreasonable interest. Some of the poor had even been forced to subject their sons and daughters to slavery to pay their debts.

Can you imagine? In the midst of trying to rally the people of Jerusalem to build this wall, Nehemiah had to deal with political nonsense and greed. But he resolved to keep on going. And in so doing, he demonstrated the first method for defeating discouragement: *refusing to allow disappointment to fester until it becomes discouragement.* Nehemiah surely was disappointed in his fellow Jews for placing a burden on the poor, but he decided to simply focus on fixing the problem and then moved forward.

Here is what happened as a result: "So the wall was completed on the twenty-fifth of the month Elul, in fifty-two days. When all our enemies heard of it, and all the nations surrounding us saw it, they lost their confidence; for they recognized that this work had been accomplished with the help of our God" (Nehemiah 6:15–16).

In spite of the obstacles he faced—attacks from his enemies, rebellion from within, and other constant opportunities for discouragement—Nehemiah completed the wall. He got the job done. At the same time, he defeated discouragement not only for himself but also for those living in Jerusalem with him.

If you want to experience this same kind of victory, you need to ask yourself the right question. The question is not, "*Can* I get out of this discouragement?" Rather, it is, "*Will* I get out of it?" Because you have the choice. You *are* going to experience disappointments in life. You do not have any say in the matter. But discouragement is a choice—it is a choice to go into it, and it is a choice to get out.

When you are heading in the direction of discouragement, confess the following to your heavenly Father. First, say, *"Lord, I know You're with me in this disappointment (or in this discouragement). I know You're with me."* Next, proclaim, *"I know You are in control of my life. You know all about what is going on and have power to change anything You choose."* Finally, say to God, *"I know that You are going to turn this around for good, and I trust you. You know my pain and my hurt, but I am looking to see how You turn this for good."* Those three truths will help you defeat discouragement every time. God is with you, is in control, and will use whatever you are facing to accomplish something good.

As you do this, you will find that you cannot confess those three truths with any kind of sincerity and remain in discouragement. The reason for this is because you are removing the attention from your disappointments and focusing it where it belongs: *on God.* Just tell Him, "Father, You haven't left me. You're in control. You're working for my benefit." All three of those statements are true. And all three of those truths will help you defeat discouragement.

9. "Trust in the Lord with all your heart, and lean not on your own understanding; in all your ways acknowledge Him, and He shall direct your paths" (Proverbs 3:5–6). How can trusting God with all your heart help you to overcome discouragement?

....

....

....

....

....

....

....

....

....

....

....

....

10. "So the wall was finished. . . . When all our enemies heard of it . . . they were very disheartened in their own eyes; for they perceived that this work was done by our God" (Nehemiah 6:15–16). What greater purpose was served as a result of Nehemiah not getting discouraged? How are others seeing God's hand in your life through the way you respond to trials?

....

....

....

....

....

....

....

....

....

....

....

....

We have now come to the end of this study on becoming emotionally whole. However, before we conclude, I believe it is worth emphasizing one more time that God is the creator of your emotions. He is the reason you are able to feel—even in those times when you might feel a little too deeply and a little too strongly. This means that you don't need to fear your feelings, for God has been with you all along this journey toward becoming emotionally whole.

Not only that, but God is also in control of all things—including your feelings. He knows how you feel and knows *why* you feel. So there's no sense hiding your feelings from Him. Finally, He is able to use all things to accomplish what is good—even including those negative emotions and feelings that seem to be out of control.

So don't try to run away from your feelings. Don't ignore them and hope they go away. Instead, as you continue forward on this journey toward a healthy emotional life, bring your emotions and your feelings to God. Share your thoughts and emotions with Him. As you do, you will be well on the way to becoming emotionally whole.

TODAY AND TOMORROW

Today: I don't have to dwell on the disappointments
I experience each day.

Tomorrow: I will defeat discouragement by turning
to God because He is with me, He is in control, and He
works all things together for good.

CLOSING PRAYER

Heavenly Father, we want to get just a glimpse of what You see in us. We want to get a glimpse of the potential we all have in becoming the men and women that You want us to be. We want to continue growing in You . . . never being satisfied in where we are. Help us to put aside feelings of discouragement. Help us to experience the hope of the incredible future that You have in store for us. Fill us with Yourself and give us a better understanding of who we truly are. Allow us to embrace our emotions and not try to run from them or hide them— for we want You to use our healthy emotions to lead other people to Christ.

NOTES AND
PRAYER REQUESTS

Use this space to write any key points, questions, or prayer requests from this week's study.

LEADER'S GUIDE

Thank you for choosing to lead your group through this Bible study from Dr. Charles F. Stanley on *Becoming Emotionally Whole*. The rewards of being a leader are different from those of participating, and it is our prayer that your own walk with Jesus will be deepened by this experience. During the twelve lessons in this study, you will be helping your group members explore the topic of emotional wholeness while using Dr. Stanley's teachings and review questions to encourage group discussion. There are multiple components in this section to help you structure your lessons and discussion time, so be sure to read and consider each one.

BEFORE YOU BEGIN

Before your first meeting, make sure your group members each have a copy of *Becoming Emotionally Whole* so they can follow along in the study guide and have their answers written out ahead of time. Alternately, you can hand out the study guides at your first meeting and give the group members some time to look over the material and ask any preliminary questions. During your first meeting, be sure to send a sheet around the room and have the members write down their name, phone number, and email address so you can keep in touch with them during the week.

To ensure everyone has a chance to participate in the discussion, the ideal size for a group is around eight to ten people. If there are more than ten people, break up the bigger group into smaller subgroups. Make sure the members are committed to participating each week, as this will help create stability and help you better prepare the structure of the meeting.

At the beginning of each meeting, you may wish to start the group time by asking the group members to provide their initial reactions to the material they have read during the week. The goal is to just get the group members' preliminary thoughts—so encourage them at this point to keep their answers brief. Ideally, you want everyone in the group to get a chance to share some of their thoughts, so try to keep the responses to a minute or less.

Give the group members a chance to answer, but tell them to feel free to pass if they wish. With the rest of the study, it's generally not a good idea to have everyone answer every question—a free-flowing discussion is more desirable. But with the opening icebreaker questions, you can go around the circle. Encourage shy people to share, but don't force them. Also, try to keep any one person from dominating the discussion so everyone will have the opportunity to participate.

WEEKLY PREPARATION

As the group leader, there are a few things you can do to prepare for each meeting:

- *Be thoroughly familiar with the material in the lesson.* Make sure you understand the content of each lesson so you know how to structure the group time and are prepared to lead the group discussion.

- *Decide, ahead of time, which questions you want to discuss.* Depending on how much time you have each week, you may not be able to reflect on every question. Select specific questions that you feel will evoke the best discussion.

- *Take prayer requests.* At the end of your discussion, take prayer requests from your group members and then pray for one another.

- *Pray for your group.* Pray for your group members throughout the week and ask God to lead them as they study His Word.

- *Bring extra supplies to your meeting.* The members should bring their own pens for writing notes, but it's a good idea to have extras available for those who forget. You may also want to bring paper and additional Bibles.

STRUCTURING THE GROUP DISCUSSION TIME

You will need to determine with your group how long you want to meet each week so you can plan your time accordingly. Generally, most groups like to meet for either sixty minutes or ninety minutes, so you could use one of the following schedules:

SECTION	60 Minutes	90 Minutes
WELCOME (group members arrive and get settled)	5 minutes	10 minutes
ICEBREAKER (group members share their initial thoughts regarding the content in the lesson)	10 minutes	15 minutes
DISCUSSION (discuss the Bible study questions you selected ahead of time)	35 minutes	50 minutes
PRAYER/CLOSING (pray together as a group and dismiss)	10 minutes	15 minutes

As the group leader, it is up to you to keep track of the time and keep things moving according to your schedule. If your group is having a good discussion, don't feel the need to stop and move on to the next question. Remember, the purpose is to pull together ideas and share unique insights on the lesson. Encourage everyone to participate, but don't be concerned if certain group members are more quiet. They may just be internally reflecting on the questions and need time to process their ideas before they can share them.

GROUP DYNAMICS

Leading a group study can be a rewarding experience for you and your group members—but that doesn't mean there won't be challenges. Certain members may feel uncomfortable in discussing topics that they consider very personal and might be afraid of being called on. Some members might have disagreements on specific issues. To help prevent these scenarios, consider establishing the following ground rules:

- If someone has a question that may seem off topic, suggest that it is discussed at another time, or ask the group if they are okay with addressing that topic.

- If someone asks a question to which you do not know the answer, confess that you don't know and move on. If you feel comfortable, you can invite the other group members to give their opinions or share their comments based on personal experience.

- If you feel like a couple of people are talking much more than others, direct questions to people who may not have shared yet. You could even ask the more dominating members to help draw out the quiet ones.

- When there is a disagreement, encourage the members to process the matter in love. Invite members from opposing sides to evaluate their opinions and consider the ideas of the other members. Lead the group through Scripture that addresses the topic, and look for common ground.

When issues arise, encourage your group to follow these words from Scripture: "Love one another" (John 13:34), "If it is possible, as much as it depends on you, live peaceably with all men" (Romans 12:18), "Whatever things are true ... noble ... pure ... lovely ... if there is any virtue and if there is anything praiseworthy—meditate on these things" (Philippians 4:8), and "Be swift to hear, slow to speak, slow to wrath" (James 1:19). This will make your group time more rewarding and beneficial for everyone who attends.

Thank you again for your willingness to lead your group. May God reward your efforts and dedication, equip you to guide your group in the weeks ahead, and make your time together in *Becoming Emotionally Whole* fruitful for His kingdom.

Also Available in the
Charles F. Stanley Bible Study Series

The Charles F. Stanley Bible Study Series is a unique approach
to Bible study, incorporating biblical truth, personal insights,
emotional responses, and a call to action. Each study draws on
Dr. Stanley's many years of teaching the guiding principles found
in God's Word, showing how we can apply them in practical
ways to every situation we face. This edition of the series has
been completely revised and updated, and includes two
brand-new lessons from Dr. Stanley.

Advancing	Experiencing	Listening	Relying on the
Through Adversity	Forgiveness	to God	Holy Spirit
9780310106555	9780310106579	9780310106593	9780310106616

Available now at your favorite bookstore.
More volumes coming soon.

Thomas Nelson
Since 1798